"This is a 'must 'for any Tea

Mana

"Used this guide in three businesses now and they treat when I work them."

- Paul Thilo.
Managing Director Ribbon Care, London and Europe

"Utilising the principles in this work we transformed a good team into an empowered high-performance unit wholly aligned to some big Goals, enabling us to take the business to new levels of excellence right across the business – You just have to use it!!"

- Dave Barker.
CEO Aquila Nuclear Engineering Ltd,
Hampshire. Part of the Calder Group of Companies.

"This is a MUST read for the busy Leader"

- Vicky Skinner.
Chief Financial Officer Urbanest, London

"You cannot make the most of your Team without perusing these principles – they work when you work them!"

- Mark Wells.
Chairman Blanchard Wells Structures & Civils,
Hampshire

"The principles in this book have helped me transform myself, my team and our Business over the past three years. They have helped build trust, alignment, and most importantly, an enjoyable place to work and I would recommend them to anyone. They have had such an impact we even named our dog Ralph!"

- Ben Collins.
Principal Partner Collins Wealth Management,
Lincolnshire

The Essential Leaders Guide - how to build a High Performing Team

By Ralph Peters

www.newgeneration-publishing.com

 New Generation Publishing

National Centre for Post-Qualifying Social Work
Bournemouth University
4th Floor, Royal London House
Christchurch Road
Bournemouth
Dorset
BH1 3LT UK
researchpqsw@bournemouth.ac.uk
www.ncpqsw.com

Contents

About the Author

Ralph graduated from the Royal Military Academy Sandhurst into the Royal Artillery. A short but really enjoyable career in the Army was followed by a move into Sales with the Save & Prosper Group where his first steps into Management were made – 11 years later he was appointed to the Main Board of Abbey Life Plc. where he had many executive experiences which included leading a Team who doubled the size and turnover of Sales in a challenging market, being a part of the Team who took the organization through an extremely positive floatation.

At the age of 39 he decided to leave Corporate life for wider experiences 'go it alone and do his own thing' by setting up and developing his own Consultancy PMC Ltd. This is when Ralph established his interest in Teams and learned the many situations and the ONE characteristic that leads to them 'finding it easier to be dysfunctional rather than functional and enjoyable to work in '! He was regularly asked to Coach Senior Executives which is what led to him working with their Teams to produce some really exciting breakthroughs which led to improved results with less stress.

From this he created processes and exercises which grow trust, alignment and an enjoyable working environment, all of which lead to high levels of positive functionality and on occasions some quite extraordinary Results. During the past five years he has created for Teams, a way of them accepting why they might be dysfunctional and addressing the issues with ease. This has led to truly enjoyable breakthroughs in cohesiveness and job satisfaction.

Ralph has enjoyed Non-Executive Director roles in the past with Cruickshank and Partners (part of BICC) and Just Retirement Assurance which have added substantially to his experience of participating in a practical way in Leadership Teams and comprehending the modern challenges that organisations face.

During the 15 years before selling PMC Ltd and the subsequent 9 years he has only worked with Senior Teams and senior Leaders in a wide range of organisations. These have and do include well known Global businesses, SME's, not for Profit as well as some enjoyable Pro Bono assignments. He is at home with a Team of Engineers or a Team of Treasury experts, a College and School leadership Team or the owners of a Contact Centre.

Whilst Ralph doesn't call Coaching Teams 'work' he has an active life beyond the workplace. There are four fantastic children (not to mention six grandchildren) who all receive some kind of connection and attention monthly. There exists a passion for Rugby as a result of which he played until his early sixties, and he has watched International Rugby in every major rugby stadium in the world. The Mountains of Scotland are where he is to be found stretching his legs weekly. His days are filled with Coaching, further learning, preparing for Team interventions and he benefits from regular meditating over the past six years.

Introduction

Times are tough. Covid 19, quantitative easing, slowing markets, downsizing, cost cutting and slower investment will all taken their toll. Their effects are prevalent in every corner of every organization. We start 'recovery' and along comes Brexit sowing further seeds of doubt. These two impacts on the business world remind me that over my many years of Corporate life there was always something that 'impacted markets' – the Falklands, Iraq, National strikes and so on. At the centre of it all are a lot less people attempting to do a lot more work, and struggling to enjoy the success they deserve.

Something has to give. We all need to find a new way of working or companies will slowly grind themselves and their teams into the ground as they run faster and faster to stay still. Quite simply, the current situation is not sustainable. We have to find 'new ways of enjoying work and achieving our Goals.

There is an answer and that answer lies in your team. The people already within your organisation are the key to success. We all have unharnessed talent and effort right in front of us in the shape of our teams and more often than not we know that and are just frustrated at not being able to fully realize it.

Never mind that each member of your workforce is already doing enough work for two people. By creating a high performing team, it is possible to get a handful of people to do the work of dozens. Forget what you were taught at school. With a high performing team, four plus four can equal ten, or even more when their focused mindsets are positive, creative and aligned.

The reason why high performing teams can produce the magic calculation of four plus four equalling ten or more is because the complimentary skills and energy of the individuals on that team exceed the sum of the parts. Plus, by creating and agreeing upon clear goals and approaches, they can support real-time problem solving. 'Real time', that is being present, controlling the controllable elements is one of the clues to a harmonious more productive way forward. Acting on initiative is encouraged because everyone in an aligned Team accepts that it is the way to overcome barriers in the way of top-class performance.

If you want to transform your business and get it back on track, you must first transform your team. If it is time to reinvent your business then first start by reinventing your Leadership Team.

When you can get everyone to work together in a powerful way and take personal responsibility for their own performance, it will generate significant and measurable improvement, every time.

High performing teams are different from ordinary teams because they have:

- A greater sense of purpose. They know what they are doing and why they are doing it.
- More ambitious performance goals.
- Mutual accountability. Everyone on the team acknowledges each other's strengths and weaknesses and helps each other towards common goals.
- More creativity in problem solving.
- Energy. The team wants to get things done.
- There is a sincere interest in each other's growth and personal improvement.

Perhaps one of the most recognizable qualities of a high performing team is all egos are left in the reception area. No one sits in their silos thinking that they are better than everyone else, or 'that's not my job'. Similarly, no one snipes from the side-lines, revelling in their colleagues' cock-ups. They just get on with it and work together to get the critical things done. Leaving ego at the door is a breakthrough waiting to happen, it is a challenge because more often than not our ego drove us to the position each Team member presently holds, however, it is a challenge worth addressing.

Does all of this sound like your current team?

If the answer is no, or more probably, 'not even close', then The Essential Leaders Guide will uncover solutions for you. In over twenty seven years of coaching teams I have helped hundreds of teams realize their full potential and become ' high performing'. I have worked with every sort of company, from not-for-profit organizations, to SMEs with profits in the small millions, to the top tier of some of the UK's leading blue chip organizations. Along the way, I have identified principles and practices which do realise amazing team performances. I have devised models of excellence for whole organisations to follow.

My extensive experience of working with teams has shown me that:

- Intent is rarely followed through without external perspective and guidance
- Vast amounts of subliminal lack of trust exists in the vast majority of teams, debilitating their true potential
- The leader's perspective is rarely mirrored by the team!

- Hidden limiting beliefs act as roadblocks to realising full potential in even the most positive of teams
- Even the most energetic of teams benefit immensely from monthly coaching - just as the sports teams benefit from continuous creative coaching.

Many of those teams I have worked with, started off riven by in-fighting and petty goal scoring and their team leaders despaired that they could even get them to stay in the same room without arguing, let alone work like a well-oiled machine. But, I have proved that it is possible and I have proved it again and again. I have constantly used experiences from both my background and from the teams that I have helped to show other teams the way forward.

The Libyan Experience

No, not the recent one. The one I am referring to is in the late 1960's when, as a potential officer in training at The Royal Military Academy Sandhurst, I was on an 'exercise' to put the previous term's infantry learning into practice in Libya. This was to be my first experience of organized disorganization and one I had often used since in my work with teams. We had endured an 18-hour delay in Nice, courtesy of the RAF omitting to pack some anti-freeze, we had been on and off the trucks ready to travel from Tripoli to Benghazi several times and then, as we were sitting in the desert at dawn, out of nowhere we were exposed to some sound learning that still holds true for team leaders today.

Sergeant Cameron, who was a staunch, upright, Glaswegian in charge of our platoon and infantry training, suddenly declared to his complaining, sleep-deprived, brood who were still awaiting their transport; "You shouldn't have joined if you can't take a joke!!". He followed that up by adopting a serious 'I'm on your side' tone and gave us some advice on the elements he saw as critical to create a high performing platoon (team). He told us:

- The journey is never a smooth one, therefore you have to be vigilant at all times
- It will test you and challenge you
- As the team leader you have to be determined. Not simply keen: determined
- You have to have decided and communicated your own version of the standards you expect (Vision and Values in today's parlance)
- You will require will power rather than 'noisy drive'!

Sergeant Cameron said to us, very seriously, that in our quest to be the best leaders that our troops deserve, we would do well to adopt the following philosophy:

- Be consciously aware and expect, as well as demand, the best of people (standards)
- Make the journey fun and interesting, rather than serious
- Show your appreciation and acknowledgement of people's honest intent and for a job well done.

I thank Sergeant Cameron for his constructive guidance back then. As I said, I have since successfully employed it with hundreds of people on my commercial journey to help teams perform to their best ability.

In The Essential Leaders Guide I have shared the benefits of my 27 years of working with high performing teams. Broken into two parts, part one looks at the six principles of a high performing team. These are the principles that, when understood and mixed in the right ways, at the right times, lead into high performing outcomes. Part two adds four extra characteristics of a high performing team into the mix. These are the additional components which will deliver the complimentary skills, understanding, commitment and traits that are essential if everyone is to succeed. They include exposing the ego and its debilitating impact on teams generally and on Senior Executive Teams in particular.

So, what are these all important principles at the centre of a high performing team?

1. **Vision.** There has to be a positive and inspiring vision of the future. It requires constant communication through behaviours as well as words of encouragement.
2. **Plan and process.** Because, if you don't know where you are going, how are you going to get there? (Or even know once you've reached your destination.)
3. **Attitude.** You know what a bad attitude can do. Now see what a good one among the whole team can achieve and its impact on the wider workforce.
4. **Alignment.** Imagine the power of everyone on the team pulling in the same direction.
5. **Values.** There is much more to values than a document framed behind the reception desk. Without true commitment to the value principle, high performing team results will not occur.
6. **Rigid flexibility.** No plan, however good will survive first contact with the outside world. But, if your team is flexible enough to think on their feet, this is not a problem.

Individually, any one of these principles, if properly pursued, would make a big difference to a team. However, the real power comes when they are all followed as a whole.

Although written sequentially, the key to part one of this book is that each one of the principles has to be embraced in tandem in order to be truly effective in creating a high performing team. Breaking it down in this way just makes each chapter easier to digest and understand.

Part two, the four characteristics and exposing the positive as well as negative impacts of the ego, are a similar case in point. Again, adopting any of the four characteristics of trust, passion, creativity and credibility, would make a positive difference. Addressing the ego alone will create real breakthroughs. But, taken as a whole, their power is exponential.

There are no 'six steps to high performing teams' – this is an integral framework which requires the Leaders constant vigilance and allows for maximum flexibility. Rather than it being a step by step approach to success it is all the ingredients for greater success and satisfaction as a leader. It provides you with the best ingredients/ tools for ensuring high performance from your unique Team in whatever form works best for you right now, with the understanding that what works best will change over time.

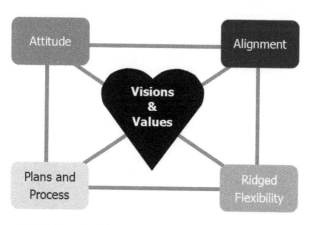

Figure 1: 'All the principles must be in play'

The power of the team leader

The chances are, if you are reading this book, you are probably in a senior position in a team and looking at how you can do better. If you've been struggling along for a while all this gung ho stuff about teams performing better than you could ever have imagined may just seem a little, well, daunting. Or, it may sound credible, but you will harbour serious doubts about whether it can really work for you.

You may think:

- I really don't want to address the elephants in the corner
- I'm not sure if I can trust my team's confidentiality
- If we spend too much time together it will provide a platform for negativity
- It will take too much time
- I don't really want to tackle the competing egos – they work well as individuals
- It is better and quicker for a few of us to decide on important issues
- I can't change the people on the team
- We have done something like this before

Some of these statements may ring true for you. You may even have other reservations. But, let's for a moment tackle these statements and turn them on their head. Let's consider the *opposite* of their sentiment. Imagine if you did address those elephants, trust your team and have them confident to trust each other openly, or tackle the negativity. What would happen then? I will tell you what will happen then; you will realize a marked improvement in performance and vocational satisfaction.

The gains to be had from creating a high performing team are:

- Greater productivity and communication with ease
- Greater speed as a result of alignment and trust
- Greater commitment to the task, the team and each other
- Higher levels of trust and willingness to positively support and hold each other accountable
- Decrease in organizational politics – releasing positive energy
- Succinct problem solving
- Deeper and consistent communication of the wider vision
- Meetings that are timely, prepared for by all and looked forward to
- Vast vocational satisfaction leading to an energy and joy currently missing from many workplaces
- Less stress and more fun
- A truly great place to work
- A real legacy of having made your people the best that they could be
- A comfortable work/ life balance

That doesn't sound such a bad thing, does it?

As a team leader you have the key to the combination that will unlock all those high performing team principles. But, there is some even better news too. In my experience, a good, committed team leader can not only pull together a high performing team to share benefits like those above, he or she can *raise* these results by a further 25 per cent.

Ah, you may be thinking, that's pretty obvious. Of course the team leader has to get in there and get their hands dirty. Again, experience tells me this is not so. I have met many team leaders who think that all they have to do is authorize a team performance programme, sign off the invoice and then sit down and await the results. They can't seem to conceptualize that they themselves have to change their way of thinking too. They do and you do too. You cannot lead the change without being part of it. The individual is, after all, where the high performing team starts. If you are a team leader at any level, then the time has come for you to play that reinventing part. You, the leader, have a huge resource and it's not in the job title or the organizational position.

When a leader gives visionary direction and accompanies it with coaching and comfort, removes fear and implied threat, focuses his or her people on the controllable, not the uncontrollable, then I know I have met a team leader who will ensure the performance breakthroughs that he or she dreams of getting from their team.

The teams that I have worked with who have transformed the fastest from $4 + 4 = 7$, to $4 + 4 = 10$ or more, were the ones where the leader was a coach and shared the leadership. He or she kept the vision and values on the agenda every day, policed open and honest communication and clarified two-way expectations. They also saw their way to managing their time with an effective balance between team members, team goals and the pressing corporate side of their role.

True team leaders not only communicate an inspiring vision of the future, they also model the way by leading the change.

What is a team?

Before we begin this journey, it may help to go back to basics and ask; what is a team?

According to HB Karp (1980), a team is a group who must work interdependently in order to attain individual and group objectives. Teams can be differentiated from other types of groups by certain characteristics. According to Reilly and Jones (1974), teams possess the following unique characteristics:

- The group must have an agreement or a reason *for working together.(Vision, Plan Values)*
- Group members must be *interdependent*, each needing one another's experience, abilities and commitment in order to reach a common goal. (sometimes a group of people , all with the same roles, and therefore not interdependent , are called a Team)
- Group members must be *committed* to the idea that working together produces more effective decisions than does working in isolation. (out of our silos)
- The group must operate as a functioning unit *within the larger organisational context.*

Having just made those points of clarity I have to challenge 'what is in a name? 'One for all and all for one is what the leader of a high performing Team needs to be encouraging. I win only when the Team wins is where we are going. Andy Murray has it, Alec Ferguson and his drive for standards had it – these 'champions' know that building a High Performance Team is not an event but and encouraging attitude and process for you to pursue . In this age of rapidly changing technology, market-driven decision-making, customer sophistication and employee restlessness, leaders and managers are constantly faced with new challenges. That is before you take into account the recent downturn and challenges of Brexit or or! Organisations must build new structures and master new skills in order to compete, survive and enjoy.

As work settings become more complex and involve increased numbers of interpersonal interactions, individual effort has less impact. In order to increase efficiency and effectiveness, a group effort is required. The creation of teams has become a key strategy in many organisations. Team building is an essential element in supporting and improving the effectiveness of small groups and task forces and must be a key part of a total programme of organisational change. A high performing Team needs less 'meetings', and has more time for the important.

What does all this tell us? Teams can and should be the critical differentiator in today's challenging times. Our people and the way they are led in teams are the only engine of power left that will enable the good to become truly outstanding.

So, if you want to make a difference in a challenged world, the answer is to create high performance teams that will create shareholder value, better results and a culture that models winning ways.

The Essential Leaders Guide shows how to create, inspire and maintain that high performing team and start making things happen.

Remember, you have a huge opportunity ahead of you to create something that will make other teams gasp in disbelief. How do you get everyone to do so much, so happily and so efficiently, they'll ask.

Here is how.

Part 1: Key principles of a high performing team

Chapter one - Vision

Imagine, if you will, a car with its wheels spinning in the mud. There is smoke rising from below, the engine is spluttering with the effort and flecks of sodden mud are flying everywhere. Then suddenly, just when the situation looks utterly hopeless, the driver shifts a gear and the car miraculously pulls away as though there had never really been a problem at all.

I have made this analogy of the car stuck in the mud and its wheels not gaining traction many times when I have been asked; what is vision? It seems every team leader has heard of this vision thing and senses that they need one, but that is as far as they go. I have met many who are clear of their Vision of the future but do not know how to lever its power – communicate it in a behavioural and inspirational way.

Metaphorically, this leader and their team are still sloshing around in the mud. Tackling the 'latest' corporate diversion !

The simple answer to this often asked question is; having a vision which has been truly understood and inspirational enough to be bought into by the whole team, is the equivalent of providing a company with a bigger gearbox. This bigger gearbox is not just good enough to help a company accelerate away with ease, it is powerful enough to see you through any sticky situation without any awkward hold-ups, making the best decisions along the way. It prevents diversions and forces innovation around the end game rather than for its own sake.

Vision is an easy and simple AND relevant discussion to be having on the front line of your Business or Organisation.

Often though, in the belief that I have clarified the matter, I ask the self-same leaders, what is your long-term vision? There are many responses to this, but it is quite likely the reply will involve an embarrassed shrug of the shoulders, or the two word answer; to survive. On the rare occasions when they do come up with something more coherent, it is seldom detailed enough to cater for all the stakeholders on their business.

Most of the time, people are too busy thinking about the present to even consider what lies ahead. Businesses are seemingly prepared to limp along from month-to-month, just getting on with things, and then wonder why they are not growing, or worse still, are going backwards. The team works harder and harder but nothing seems to change. Everyone becomes frustrated and fed up at this lack of progress, but no one can understand why the business seems stuck fast. This is 'action without vision' in action! Rushed meeting to rushed meeting chasing the short term – any space for thought , peace , is taken up by e mails!

The answer to why nothing seems to change, however hard the team works is blindingly obvious, if people would only look.

No team can strive to reach a goal , valuable long term sustainable business if they don't know what that goal is or what it looks and feels like.

Ironically, the best they can do without a proper vision is 'survive', but where is the point in that? Without a well-conceived, continuously reinforced, inspirational vision of the future, the far corners of the workforce won't know what to do to make the difference that the company leadership wants to see happen. Worse still, they will probably take the option to 'self-serve' because they will see work as 'only a job'. In other words, in the absence of having a greater ideal, they will unconsciously disengage from the company and concentrate on looking after number one. That is human nature, but without vision, who could blame them?

I once met with a CEO and Operations Director of a UK based organisation who told me that he was really concerned about the lack of fresh thinking in his firm. He told me in great detail about the problems caused by the silo mentality of his team, who resolutely concentrated on their own little part of the equation. He was utterly fed up that everyone around him put business as usual ahead of the organisation's longer term future.

When I asked this executive about his company's vision of the future, he pointed out very proudly the fact the business had held a one day workshop on vision and had produced a very attractive document. However, that was as far as they went. There had been no attempt to share the vision, or engage the workforce. They had taken the process no further than the original workshop and had crucially missed out on coming up with any behavioural examples for the team to relate to. In short, they had completely wasted their time, reminding me that ' nothing changes in a workshop'.

Look at it another way. If you don't share your vision with the team (or don't have one), it is the equivalent of saying to someone I will give you a million pounds if you can chop down this forest today and here is an axe and a saw. It is not even a chainsaw. If they work their fingers to the bone, they are never, ever going to do it. Do you know why? Because they don't have the right tools. It is just the same if you ask your team to work their socks off – but don't give them the bigger picture, the tools, the understanding to achieve what you ask. This leads to a challenging and frustrating environment – Vision in Action removes frustration!

A powerful vision will harness and focus all of the energy, innovation and effort of the team and channel it into helping a company get where it wants to be both now and in the longer term. Teams who grasp the power of vision don't just thrive. In my experience they achieve the potentially impossible. They will also show their competitors a clean pair of wheels, while others are still floundering around in the mud wondering how are they doing so well ?

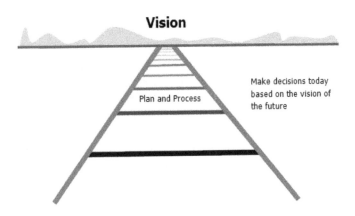

Figure 2: 'Vision without action is merely a dream'
We need vision because:

- It helps us look to the future of our business in a *positive* way

- It defines the *basics* from which we can develop our organisations for the future...
- ..and gives more *meaning* to the present
- It gives the whole team a *common language* to discuss the future in a practical and specific way
- It shows each individual on the team how their own *personal contribution* can make a difference to that future
- It puts 'business as usual' in perspective
- It provides the basis for pertinent ' Coaching conversations' at all levels

Those who say they just want 'to survive' might think that they don't have the capacity or the time to think about the future. But, this is exactly why they need a vision. Having a positive vision for the future is one of the most powerful motivating forces there is.

All the greatest leaps forward in history, from the Seven Wonders of the World, to more modern advancements such as computers, the space shuttle, the telephone and the iPhone were all once just an idea in someone's head. Somebody sat down and dreamed of how they could make the future better. Then, with a lot of trial and error, that person made that vision real or harnessed the efforts of others to realise the desired inspirational future

On many, if not all, of these occasions, these truly great historical advancements succeeded against all the odds. Now, we all know that for every great achievement, many other dreams will have fallen by the wayside, even if they were technically, creatively or architecturally, just as brilliant, if not more so. So, why do some succeed and others fail? The reason is, the person who had that original vision somehow found a way to articulate it to people around them and ignite the passion of others to support that vision. Then, with that support, they made the vision a reality. That is the difference between being great and being still in there as an also ran.

I was once an executive director responsible for sales at an insurance company. As an insider it was not hard to see that administration was poor, the company was anything but customer friendly and the whole operation was cost inefficient. The impression was pretty poor from the outside too and, in fact, it got so bad that the national press were writing an ever growing number of disparaging articles about us.

Then, one January, the chief executive stood up to tell us everything was going to change. When he announced his vision of the future to 2,000 head office workers there was quite a lot of head scratching. I'm sure that quite a few people thought he had gone completely mad when he said his vision was to see customers willingly praising the administration at the firm and salespeople openly boasting that they worked there. At the end of his rousing talk, which was stuffed full of the behavioural examples he wanted to see (none of which were close to the current reality), the CEO rounded it all off with a summary he called 'two days to Christmas'. By the close of that year, he wanted 95 per cent of all customer and new business enquiries to be responded to within 48 hours. This was miles away from the present yet something everyone could grasp.

That was his inspiring vision. The CEO backed-up his initial statement with a programme of continuous and relentless communication. Engagement with the team became the norm.
What was the outcome? Mountains *were* moved. Staff rose to the occasion by achieving a 95.4 per cent turnaround of customer and new business enquiries within

two days by November. Once they met that goal, they went on to get better and better.

We're not all going to invent something as ground-breaking as the World Wide Web, or build breath-taking monuments which will entrance generation after generation to come. However, we can all harness the tremendous power of vision and use it to drive our organisations to a position above all others in their field.

Think of all the companies you really admire, or which have been consistently successful. I'll bet you a pound to a penny they are all being driven by a really powerful vision.

Consider the following visions from the past, as an example:

- British Airways – The World's favourite airline (without Government financial backing)
- IBM – Solutions for a small planet
- Microsoft - There will be a personal computer on every desk running Microsoft software
- Nokia – Connecting people
- Xerox – The document company

What did these companies all have in common? You can clearly see what they are trying to achieve – and they are doing it.

Having a vision can have a positive impact on all aspects of your life. Many years ago, when I sat down to give real thought to my vision for the future, I realised that what made me happiest was a particular area in Scotland, which I loved. I'm no artist, but I got out a piece of paper, sat down and drew my vision which incorporated this beautiful vista of this area, my family and my own business, in this case represented by a sketch of my laptop.

Connecting with clients. My vision for the future, which I carefully placed on the wall of my office, was to have a different balance and pace to my life in the future working with teams commercially and pro bono. I also wanted to have an impact on my children and future grandchildren's lives. I know that vision works. **The proof?** While I am writing this the stunning view from my study window is of Loch Fyne! Parts of my vision are already realised. Technology allows me to be in touch with clients face to face daily if necessary.

Some years after I sketched my original vision, I sold my business and was weighing up what to do with my money. One Sunday, I spotted a wonderful ski chalet being advertised for sale in the Sunday papers. I was on the verge of picking up the phone to speak to the agent, when I stopped myself short. I remembered my vision and that sketch which had been on the wall of my office for all those years, egging me on. Had I bought this chalet, I would never have been able to buy the plot of land, which I subsequently bought in my favourite area of Scotland. I would never have realised the vision that has since bought great happiness to both me and my family and many visitors to our peaceful spot.

I have proved, on both a personal and business level, that vision really does allow you to make better decisions in the moment.

A vision is not about….

- Becoming the *fastest* widget-maker in the world
- Hoping to be the *best-loved* company in your field
- Pledging to deliver a *better product or service* to your customers on a consistent basis

It's amazing. Despite being one of the most over-used words in the corporate lexicon, very few people actually understand what a vision actually is. Most businesspeople (at least the ones who are not just planning 'to survive') have latched on to the fact that it is about highlighting some sort of quality or attribute that their company has that makes it stand out from the crowd. However, they think that if they can make some sort of lofty statement about a company's current reason for being, that's the vision bit ticked off. They'd be completely wrong.

A vision is nothing to do with what a company is currently getting right. Or, thinks it is getting right. It is not some highly generic statement, hoping to be the best, or fastest, or biggest. It is not highly speculative.

The following statement, for example, is not a true vision:

Acme Corp's vision is to be the world leader in digital widgets and related services, earning our customer's enthusiasm through continuous improvement, innovation and the commitment of our first class team.

It is too full of non-exclusive phrases and words such as 'enthusiasm' and 'innovation' are wide open to a range of interpretations. This describes nothing about what the company really wants to do and be in the future, or how. Being 'number one' or 'world class' are great sentiments, but they don't make a vision. In order for a vision to become a reality, it has to be precise enough that anyone it touches can immediately recognize his or her place in that vision and the part they can play.

Similarly, the following is not a vision:

To increase profit by 20% by the year 2025

Visions are not expressed in numbers. Numbers, be it profit, turnover, or employing two million staff, are a *consequence* of achieving that vision. Figures are actually particularly distracting because they are simply a marker to show how successful a company has been, but tell you absolutely nothing about how or why it ever managed it.

So, lesson one, never put figures or vague aspirations into a vision.

A vision is….

- A short, succinct and inspiring statement about what a company hopes to be and as a result achieve in the future.
- Positive and inspiring
- Specific and provocative, referring directly to an organisation's winning idea or whatever makes it different from its competitors.
- About a way of 'being' that will be attractive to all stakeholders

Most of all, a vision is:

Challenging

Everyone must see that they will have to stretch their skills to the upmost capacity, even beyond what they have ever thought they could achieve, in order to realize the vision. To improve performance , behaviour at all levels needs to shift.

As an exercise, why not write down the one you have in your mind for your company right now, or maybe the one you're already using. Is it what you would like your customers, your employees, your suppliers and your industry to be saying about you in five years' time? Does it actually mean anything to you, or those stakeholders, at all?

Then, cover your company's name up and insert the name of your biggest competitor and see if it means anything now. I'll be prepared to lay a small wager that the vision statement you are looking at is so generic it could stand for half a dozen companies in your sector.

Finding your company's vision

Looking forward three to five years, if you could have anything you ever wanted for your company, what would it be? Be as greedy as you like. I have helped Team Leaders and CEOs create their inspiring Vision of the future by asking them to relax and imagine that they had been away from their business for up to five years and on their return they met and spoke to the Leadership Team, Customers (internal and external), to a wide range of Staff , and if pertinent suppliers and share holders. Then I ask the individual to write down how each of the Stakeholders described what it is like here in amazingly glowing terms – his dream response in other words . That is a Vision.

Some people might answer; I want to have the best products. Others might say, I'd like it to be a great place to work. The most common response is; I want to increase turnover and profit by £x million.

None of these are real visions (and remember – no numbers are allowed). They are vague ambitions and tell us nothing specific about your company and how it is working. So, let's start again. This time, let's bring in some members of your team to help us.

Ask each one individually to imagine that the person at the head of the company has been away from the business for three to five years. Everyone has been given carte blanche to do everything that they have always wanted to do in order to improve their own particular sector in the best interests of the organisation. During that time, the company has gone from strength to strength. Can they each specify what has happened in their own department to bring about this magnificent progress?

Thus, the human resources manager may say that staff turnover has plummeted from 22 per cent a year to just 6 per cent, thanks to a policy of allowing home working, relaxing the formerly strict dress code and introducing regular team social events. The R&D team may say that increased investment has brought about a 20 per cent boost to successful new product innovations. Meanwhile, the operations manager may describe how product reliability has soared thanks to closer monitoring of the supply chain and involving the Supervisors in Lean management thinking.

Now, we are getting somewhere.

If you put all of those ideas up on a white board you would be quickly able to see the gap between what your company is now and what it could be. It shows you a snapshot of what your company can be at its very amazing best. That list of statements is the basis for defining your vision.

Now you have this basis and everyone is visualising the heights the company can reach, it is time to probe deeper. Using the previous ideals listed on your white board, consider:
- What will the company be famous for?
- What will competitors say about you?

- How would those envious rivals describe your team?
- What will customers say when they discuss your products with their peers?
- Who will be vying to become your business partners?

Your job now is to condense this down into an inspiring, pithy statement that means something specific to your company and use the wider answers to communicate continuously with your workforce.

Getting ready to apply that vision

Most people who've made it this far might, by now, be feeling pretty pleased with themselves. And, so you should. But the process doesn't end here.

Until a vision is shared with the whole team that is, the whole organisation, and they all agree to support it, it really isn't worth the paper it is written on. I have seen a number of organisations boasting that they have a vision, yet this vision is barely viewed on a regular basis and it is rare to see day-to-day activities aligned towards the apparently inspiring vision of the future. It simply ticks the box of having a vision and stops dead in its tracks. They might as well not have bothered.

The answer, however, does not lie in putting the vision statement in large lettering in a frame behind the reception desk, or pasting it prominently in the annual report, or applying it as a companywide screen saver. That will just become wallpaper after a time, as any marketing person will tell you if you ask them about the billboard effect. Nothing wrong with doing these things but they are only a supportive start to the process of marching directly towards your Vision of the future.

No, the challenge is, to get everyone, from the car park attendant to the board to buy into the vision and start taking the bold steps to behave it.

Once you have a vision, you've merely settled on the direction. Until everyone heads off in that direction, the vision has no chance of becoming a reality. There are, after all, two ways of working at a company. One is for everyone to turn up on time, do their job, go home and then get paid. The other way is for everyone to turn up early because they are excited and motivated, do their job while interacting with people at all levels because they know where their ship is going, and then go home excited and motivated that each of them know how to 'make a difference'. Which scenario would you prefer for your team? I know which one will produce a more successful and far reaching business. Hand on heart, so do you.

It is only 'vision with action' that is going to change your world. When vision is used to its most motivational extent, it is an empowering source of energy for staff and the senior team. It helps everyone make better decisions, easier and faster because they have all bought into and understood what the inspiring end-game is.

High performing teams need their leaders to set the direction by creating, engaging and communicating a vision which is:

- Exciting, inspiring and stated in positive terms
- Conveyed to the team and discussed at length
- Constantly emphasised and reinforced
- Brought to life through real-life behavioural examples

- A basis for challenging each other to perform for the greater good of us all

So get everyone together and tell them about the vision. Then, go on telling them, again and again and again. Use every Bulletin, quarterly, monthly meeting to remind everyone of it and request their input.

Ask each individual department to set a series of short-term goals that will go towards reaching the destination set out by the vision. They will be so delighted that there is some sort of goal that at last has meaning that they will probably be falling over themselves to put forward ideas of how to help reach it. Everyone should get involved too – don't pigeonhole ideas on a department-by-department basis. If you all work together, it is amazing what you can achieve.

If customer service is the focus for the future, there should be a company-wide discussion around the gap between the way customers think of you today, and the goal you have for the future. Contributions could and should come from everywhere.

Then, proper, in-depth analysis is required. In the customer service example here, this may entail looking closely at any customer feedback surveys to find out what people do or don't like about your company now. What do you think it would take to change any negative opinion into a positive glowing report? How would you go about achieving that?

Now you have the vision, it is far easier for both you and the team to set out the stages that need to be achieved in order to reach that goal. Plus, you can and should continually return to that vision to assess if you are any closer to realising that dream. If you are not, then you need to start looking very closely at why not.

Part of the beauty of vision is that as it is expressed in terms of a three or five year plan, it is a long way off. Yet, it is a brilliant framework from which to develop strategic goals and plans for the short and long term. Moving forward is no longer a blind extension of where everyone has just been, but a manageable step-by-step move towards a valuable long-term goal.

Teams will truly engage in developing and working daily towards an inspiring vision of the future. They will build their annual goals from that position guaranteeing a challenging engaging career for them and better and more consistent goal achievement for their business.

Ditch the limiting mind-sets

Your office is probably full of some pretty smart people. Of course it is, you selected them. I'm sure most, if not all, of the senior team has a string of professional qualifications, extensive experience in the industry and some valuable skills to offer. So, why is it that you can't just give them the vision and tell them to get on with it?

Because everyone, even the best and smartest among us, have limiting mind-sets.

Your team probably don't even realise that they have limiting mind-sets, but they do and they are stopping them (and your company) from reaching their full potential in performance, profit and productivity.

Limiting mind-sets stop every one of us reaching our goals in all areas of our lives. I am, as anyone who has worked with me will attest, a huge rugby fan. I find it hard to get through any of my team sessions without at least one reference to my favourite sport. If you don't share my passion, please forgive me, but I think the following story is a perfect illustration of why many visions often don't make it past the carefully crafted statement stage.

When Clive Woodward took over as coach of the England Rugby side in 1997, he asked each of his players what it was that they believed was preventing them from ever becoming world champions. He got back numerous different answers, showing numerous different limiting mind-sets as to how they couldn't or wouldn't be good enough to be world class. Together these negative responses all added up to one thing; Clive Woodward would not reach his personal goal of seeing England lifting the Rugby World Cup, until he got everyone to forget those limiting mind-sets and unite around the positive enabling vision.

Every team has limiting mind-sets. You just need to find out what they are in your team.

I always ask businesses I deal with to detail their own problems in getting the job done and discuss which, out of all of those limiting mind-sets is most holding the company back from realising its vision. I find that if you address the most pressing negative problem on the team, the other limiting mind-sets will fade as the way forward to the vision suddenly becomes clearer and more achievable.

I'll give you an example.

I once worked with an organisation full of very bright advisors. Their vision was to influence policy at the highest level through their well thought through research.

But, when I went to see them, they said it just wasn't happening. Indeed, it wasn't even close to being realised.

I asked them to define exactly why they thought they were not getting through. Well, they said, they would spend weeks and weeks preparing complex briefing papers, but when the board met they never bothered to read those papers beforehand thus rendering them fairly obsolete. So, by the time any issues were under discussion, it was too late to bring in the facts from the carefully crafted briefs. The advisors believed the board had made some pretty stupid decisions because it was not using all the available facts at its disposal. But, do you know what? Not one of them had done anything to address this problem.

I sat down with the group of frustrated advisors and asked them; what would brilliant look like? What would you really like to change? After all, at that moment they were systematically producing papers and sending them out, all the while knowing that they were never going to be read in time to make a difference. Something had to give.

Working together, the team of advisors agreed that they needed to find different way of communicating with the board. They needed to shift their 'this just doesn't work' mind set to 'we are influencing a positive difference' one. They tried a lot of different things and the one that worked was going directly to the chief executive and gently explaining their wasted productivity in producing all this work. They asked him, is there a better way of giving you these papers? There was, and together they found a really effective way to make sure the briefing papers got proper prior scrutiny.

Now, this all might sound really obvious, but this sort of acceptance of a poor situation goes on every day in corporate life. It will go on happening too and seriously

34

hold back the development of the vision, until a team takes the time to recognise their own limiting mind-set just as these advisors did. Up until then, no one had thought to challenge how they might change this frustrating and wasteful state of affairs. Once they did though, it changed everything, paving the way for them to realise their vision addressing the limiting mind set as a daily thing.

Taking ownership

One of the most common limiting mind-sets is for people to view things only from their department's limited sphere of operation.

The standard structure of most organisations is that the various departments zealously guard their own disciplines and get on with doing 'their' jobs. Thus, the sales director doggedly pursues their sales target above any other consideration, the human resources department valiantly tries to recruit, train and motivate the team, and the marketing department gets on with the communications and advertising side of things. Manufacturing and Production slave away fastidiously daily keeping things running and striving to hit wild deadlines. Each department views every other as a distraction to their own aims rather than ' we are part of the whole'.

The syndrome of 'you are responsible for this, you get it sorted' is rife for conflict, petty politicking and selfish behaviour which can blight an entire company. Occasionally, all sides will meet and may even pay lip-service to working as a team, but in reality, woe betide anyone who steps outside of their job description and is seen to 'interfere' in something that is not seen to be their direct concern.

This sort of hierarchical, self-serving, behaviour might have worked well in a Victorian factory, but it has no place whatsoever in a modern workforce. Every department needs to work together in order for the vision to succeed. The Vision should be the first topic on every Business Agenda.

The beauty of having a well thought through vision is everyone in the company takes ownership of what it is you are trying to achieve. If it is done well and communicated effectively, the grand vision will mean something to everyone and give them a reason to work together for the greater good.

With a vision, it will no longer simply be the human resources job to keep the workforce happy, or the customer relations department's task to look after those pesky customers while everyone else gets on with their 'real' jobs. Maufacturings life can be made easier and more productive when 'the whole' considers the Visions end game together. Once everyone has bought into the dream for the future, you will be amazed how quickly they will start working together to realise the vision. Suddenly it will be as though the mists have lifted. It will be clear what they are trying to achieve. Together the team can be a formidable force – together , three plus three starts to add up to eight !

Then, once the senor team has 'got it' the vision will easily cascade down the organisation. Everyone will see what change looks like. In their book Effective Leadership, Kouzes and Posner outline five researched characteristic of highly effective Leaders. One of those characteristics is termed 'Model the Way'. Effective Leaders do / behave the way they want others to behave, they model an attitude they want to see pervading their organisation or part of the organisation.

All people are boss watchers. As soon as the boss starts working differently, they will. If he or she kicks off a department meeting by saying; 'before we start, who has seen something happening in the last fortnight that they really want to highlight as being part of the vision', everyone will starting thinking in those terms too. They will be forced to constantly think about the real business now. They may say; I am sorry, I can't think of anything this time boss. But, you can bet they'll be looking out for it for the next fortnight and beyond. If they can think of something that is highlighting the enactment of the vision next time around, this is the time for praise because then you are really getting somewhere.

A strong vision becomes an all-encompassing direction for the whole organisation, not just for individual departments to struggle with (and probably retire defeated).

One method I have always found effective, and which I used in my own company, was to print off a huge poster, with the vision written in bold lettering at the top and blank below. This poster was placed in a prominent place at the beginning of every month and everyone was invited to write down examples of the vision in action whenever they saw it. You'd be amazed how keen people on the team are to put their examples down. It doesn't matter if it is a multi-million pound contract, or a small customer services triumph. It is all-important and should all go up on the board. The only rule is; figures are not allowed because every step towards realising the goal, however small, is equally important.

That is how you get the vision down into the organisation. If everyone on the team knows that there is something happening, they will start to think more about what they are doing and why they are doing it. When you can see that happening, that's a pretty exciting moment.

How vision helps us to reach our goals

Without a well-conceived, continuously reinforced, inspirational vision of the future, the far corners of your workforce won`t know what to do to make the difference of which they are capable that leadership want to see happen. Yes, everyone knows roughly where the firm wants to be, they may even have the benefit of an annual plan or strategic statement, but has everyone got the same understanding, even of those limited goals? More importantly, is everyone working their socks off in pursuit of utterly different and possibly opposing aims?

Having a well thought through and communicated vision will harvest all that energy and innovation. It will stretch the team and invigorate it so that by working together the business can achieve goals which have never before thought possible.

It is not over egging it to say, a vision can make the difference between sinking without trace, with the resultant job losses, and becoming number one in your field. I vividly remember my work with one construction company in the summer of 2007. The CEO had only been in situ for just over a year, but was becoming increasingly concerned that each year was turning out to be the same old thing. There was little creativity in the firm and some trends in their market looked like they could be a serious financial threat. By creating a three year vision and then painstakingly pursuing that vision with tenacity the company was able to completely turn itself around and prepare itself for the tough times ahead, which, as history has shown did indeed come for every company in the world thanks to the credit crunch. With one watchful eye on that powerful vision, the firm was restructured, new markets were opened up living the Values of Safety, Quality First and Right First Time and customer

relations were turned around from poor to interested again –
all through constantly reminding all of the positive Vision of
the Future.

If ever there was a case for `living the vision` this is it.
Without one I, and more importantly that CEO, knows that
at least 50% of the organisation would have been closed
down and indeed, the company may never have survived
the financial crisis at all.

Having a vision is not just about 'surviving'. It is about
finding a better place to be. The particular Company as I
write has more than doubled its workforce who are positive
and engaged and the two 'bottom lines' of turnover and profit
are now almost ten times bigger – yes ten times !

PRACTICAL GUIDE TO LEVERAGING the POWER of VISION in a TEAM:

- There are combined intellectual and emotional benefits to a high performing team of having and utilising an inspiring vision of the future.
- A vision is only of value if it is developed and initiated in detailed terms which will stretch a team.
- That vision must be exciting, inspiring and stated in positive terms.
- The Lead Team must discuss the vision at length, buy into it wholeheartedly and then consistently and persistently model the way for the whole company.
- For Vision to realise a competitive advantage for your organisation it must be continuously reinforced – it is a force for good so create the reinventing new practice of using it somewhere daily; yes daily!
- Find ways weekly of giving meaning to the present 'discussion' in the context of your inspiring corporate Vision (after all you are attending a lot of meetings which will present you with this opportunity !).
- When there are tough decisions to make, relate them to the Vision – you will not go wrong.
- Keep reminding your reports where business as usual fits with Vision AND use Vision to exit inappropriate business as usual rituals.
- Continually reinforce this powerful 'raison d'etre.

Chapter two - Plan and process

I've got something very important to tell you. It might well stop you in your tracks, but here goes.

Team building exercises don't work

I know this will surprise a lot of people reading this book. You've probably picked it up because you earnestly want to improve your team, its performance and enjoyment in making it the best it can be. It stands to reason there will be one of those gung ho exercises in here somewhere where the team has to bond while carrying a block of ice over a mountain. Or, at the very least, an exhortation to get various members of the team to fall backwards into one another's arms in an effort to learn trust.

You won't find anything like that here. There are two key reasons for that.

1. Team building away-days can be completely counterproductive. People generally (and quite understandably) hate going through these highly contrived, touchy feely, exercises with colleagues they don't trust. If you think about it, the irony of the situation shines through too because you can't build trust with a technique participants don't trust.

2. Team-building events usually happen in a retreat-style setting away from the office and involve exercises completely unrelated to the team's sphere of work. Unfortunately, while it could be made into a pleasant, fun, day out with a bit of careful management, it will not relate back to the

workplace in any transformational way. The team may well joke together when they are building a raft out of spaghetti, but will they still be joking together in a crunch meeting in three months' time? A few pleasant memories might even be created, but, in terms of creating a mutually supporting, interdependent team, it will not make one iota of difference. If you add alcohol into the mix, you may just make a bad situation a whole lot worse in the bar in the evening.

Apart from anything else, in a situation where team-building sessions like these are seen to be an urgent requirement, it is usually a symptom of a far greater malaise. Trying to replace 'bad behaviour' with 'good behaviour' just tackles the symptoms. The root cause of the problem still exists.

If a team has a lack of leadership, or direction, or values, these problems can only be fixed by solving these critical issues. Key to doing this is to introduce some plan and process.

Helping a team to see where they have come from and, more importantly, where they are going will be more valuable than a dozen away days.

I know this from bitter experience learned in my first commercial job on leaving the army. I was selling life assurance on a commission-only basis. The job kicked off with a two week induction course, two thirds of which was on sales skills and the rest of which concentrated on product. What my new employer had already established was that there was a proven routine of activities which, when pursued with the right amount of skill and positive intention, would lead to success. In a way, it was rather like a recipe and I am pleased to say my first few life assurance dishes came out near perfect. Why? Because I followed the recipe, or process, to the letter.

As I became more successful, I started to believe or as we will learn later, my ego started to believe that I knew better. So I strayed from the proven process and begun to add in an increasing number of my own interpretations. The result? A complete disaster. My sales results plummeted. No one wanted my dish.

There can be no high performing team without a process and a plan. It is impossible to realise the full potential of a group of people who are mutually responsible and interdependent, if process is not central to the team's philosophy. Process can, even must, be challenged from time to time but you have to have one in the first place. It is where you record commitment responsibility and data regarding progress.

You won't find that process doing any of those fabricated team-building days. But, you do need to get your team working together to evolve the plan.

We need plan and process because:

Processes are a series of activities which have a start point and an end point. In a high performing team process:

- Defines organisational and operational boundaries within which the team is expected to operate.
- Stops energy sapping and time wasting turf wars over what the team should be focussing on.
- Spells out the importance of tasks and the time commitment required to complete those tasks regularly

- Sets out the resources available to the team which will help it meet its goals.
- Reinforces the management support and commitment to the team in their pursuit of the key objectives.
- Keeps you on track
- Provides a positive template for wider than this Team communication as to ' how we are doing'

The process plan defines a team's mission, the scope of operations, objectives, time frame and the potential consequences. It is a crucial factor in giving a high performing team the direction to succeed. Most of the client Teams I have worked with have commented to the effect that "whilst this approach did not sound inspiring to start with they now look forward to it because it causes a focus on the Important. In fact a Team in the construction industry in 2008/9 requested, for budget reasons to decrease our half day reviews during the year to four. At the first review at the end of March one of the Directors and a major shareholder said "this is not working for us Ralph – we need to go back to Monthly!"

When people know what needs to be done, how it will be best achieved and how they will know that they have done it, life is simple and indeed more enjoyable.

Your Plan is a map, a target, a focus, a joint direction, a path. It says you are going to do something, be somewhere and be there by a certain time. Of course not all Plans work out, but without one, almost anything will turn up.

A plan and process is not....

...A detailed road map that will take a team step-by-step through what needs to be done for the next year. It does have focus on the important and it is typically very challenging.

Team leaders often get confused about plans and processes. Although they have made the important first step to realize that this is a vital element towards progress, very often they get so enthused by the idea that they go for overkill.

The first rule of plans and process is; a high performing team must only focus on three or four key results areas. Anything else is superfluous and probably won't end up getting done anyway.

Here is why.

In one of my early consultancy jobs, I worked with an IT company which had meticulously written out its plan for the budgeting process for the coming year. They were very proud indeed of that plan and had even presented it in a perfect bound book. The book was one and a half inches thick.

My somewhat over-zealous clients had agreed an annual goal and then examined every last detail of what needed to be done to achieve that goal. They then inserted that detail into a precise day-by-day planner.

I asked the team leader a question. Had he, I asked, ever heard that old military saying that no plan ever survives first contact with the enemy?

It turns out he had. However, he still didn't quite see the relevance in this case.

Well, I explained, when this plan goes 'live' things will change. External things this team may never have even imagined will happen and will have an influence. Then the changes will change. Then the changed changes will change. And so on. The possibilities for variance on the original plan are infinite.

How does all that fit in with the perfect bound plan?

The plan is a compass, not a road map. It shows the team the direction it is going and the key results areas that need to be achieved to get there. However, it needs to be flexible enough to allow for change according to the circumstance. I will explain the theory of rigid flexibility later in this book, but suffice to say, it is vital at this stage to remember that things will change. However, as long as everyone is sure of what they want to achieve, and are all working towards achieving the same thing, they will all get there in the end.

**Cultural Goals
+
Key Result Area
(KRA) goals**

Figure 3: 'A good plan is a compass **and** a combination of KRAs and cultural goals'

Plan and process is…

…about focusing on a handful of key result areas for any 12 month period or indeed every six months.

I'd like you to do an exercise for me. Let's call it 'big rock'.

Imagine a medium sized jar and beside it are some sand, some gravel, some pebbles and a pint jug filled with water. I'd like you to get it all into the jar.

Most people, after grappling with all the ingredients, will find it won't all fit. Indeed, if you try to cram it all in, it probably won't.

But, here is the secret:

The only way to make it all fit is to put in all the bigger pebbles first. Then, take the smaller ones and shake the jar a little. The smaller ones will obligingly snuggle in between the larger ones. Then, pour in the sand and, once again, give it a shake. The sand will accommodatingly fill all the gaps. Finally pour in the water and, miraculously, it will all fit.

What this fiendish metaphor is trying to show us is: you need to do the big rocks first. The big rocks in this context are the key results areas, which, if you get them right, everything else will follow.

Your KRAs could be any from the following list, or indeed others you may work through for yourself:

- Audit
- Budget
- Consultation
- Culture
- Customer Satisfaction
- Innovation
- Marketing

- Sales
- Stakeholder Perception
- Systems
- Third Party Relationships
- Transformation Plan

Taking one of these key results areas, let's say 'innovation'; let me show you how this might work.

The team at ABC Construction decide that one of the key results area for the team is innovation. Using this as a starting point, the trail of thought might go:

- We haven't innovated for ages.
- What are we good at?
- We are good at digging holes and filling them with concrete.
- What other sector needs large holes dug and filled with concrete?
- What about wind farms? With all the interest in environmentally friendly energy sources, this is a rapidly growing area. And they need very big holes for their turbines.
- OK then, how do we go about tackling that market?

Once a team can focus on an area, like innovation in the example above, they will start working together more effectively. The common goal of innovation, or whichever other KRA they chose, will create an atmosphere of ownership. Ownership is a powerful emotion and an essential component of a high performing team.

Finding your team's plan and process

The comments that opened the chapter notwithstanding, tackling plan and process is best kicked off with an off-site, away day, meeting.

Why? Because you need to get the team away from the distractions of their day-to-day roles and into an atmosphere where they can rigorously discuss a plan which will affect the whole future of the company.

But, this off-site is not for games. It is time for the team to get their heads down and really decide what is what - that can be fun as well as an opportunity for leaders to show appreciation.

Stage one – Back to basics

Before a team can begin to thrash out its plans, it has to go back to basics. Time must be devoted to finding out any negative behaviours or perceptions in the team which could stymie the process before it even begins.

Here is a great way to do just that:

Ask the team to visualise in their own minds what it is that is currently standing in the way of the team. They don't have to write anything down, just keep it in their heads.

The sort of things they may be imagining are:

- We are not getting enough sales
- The company is too slow to open accounts
- We don't have enough retail outlets
- We set budgets but never make anything like the profit that is forecast

Next, ask them to write down how they see their own role in contributing to these negative results. Even though these comments will be kept anonymous, many people will find this admission particularly tough. Some may even try to wriggle out by writing; "I don't know". That is, of course, not acceptable. Insist on full answers, however uncomfortable it makes people feel. These are things they are doing or indeed not doing which contribute to the negative result.

Once everyone has done this, gather up the notes and write them all up on a flip chart that is visible to the whole room. Remind everyone that the comments are still non-attributable.

The list on the chart will be very revealing. There are likely to be many similar or overlapping areas, which will reveal where the real problems lie in the organisation. Plus, even with a brief glance, it will not take a huge leap of imagination to identify the scope of the negative elements people visualised in the first part of the exercise.

The final stage in the exercise, and perhaps the most telling, is to ask people to write down how they justify their own negative behaviour. What excuses do they give themselves for not doing or omitting to do what they had previously written down.

Due to the negative nature of the questions here then you should be getting negative statements, for example:

- It's just not worth it
- The bosses never pay attention anyway
- There is never enough time
- Our cries for help are always ignored

The responses you have, which again should be written up on your flip-chart, will identify all the limiting mind-sets on the team. In this simple exercise you will be able to demonstrate to everyone involved that the team is carrying around a lot of negative baggage. It is this baggage that is preventing everyone from doing their job wholeheartedly. This baggage is preventing them from moving on to the next stage.

There is not a team in the world that does not have limiting mindsets. Not one. But, there is little point asking them; what are your hang-ups? They would never tell you. However, by walking them through an exercise like this they will inadvertently tell you all you need to know and more importantly what they need to discuss, acknowledge and accept.

The best way to conclude this stage by initiating a discussion as to which of the negative behaviours is most holding back the team- this may take some time to align on a single topic.

This exercise will not, of course, instantly correct these limiting mindsets. But, they will initiate a discussion of what a positive mindset could be that would be the reverse or opposite of what currently exists. It will give the team something to measure its progress against in the future.

A recent example of a team's most damaging limiting mindset was that they believed they "cannot win with this structure" (and were not directly empowered to change it). Their new empowering mindset is "We are delivering our new goals within this structure" – it isn't what they believed but it is what they worked at believing and it did produce a breakthrough in focus, results and enjoyment.

Most importantly, it will demonstrate to all concerned that the team is evolving from a group of people into a team with shared commitment and belief.

Once you discover the roadblocks that are stopping you all reaching your goals, it is time to go the next stage.

Stage two – Agreeing the key results areas

Taking the work that you have already done on vision, which was outlined in the previous chapter, now is the time to agree the key results areas.

Remind the team that in three to five years, we want to achieve X, Y and Z in order to realise our vision of the future, remind them what each of our stakeholders will be saying about how we are behaving and performing. Throw out the challenges:

What is it that we need to be doing in order to deliver that?

Which areas are our priorities during the first 6 to12 months of our visionary objectives?

A food manufacturer I was working with initially felt they should have loads of Key Result Areas but they were confusing their departmental Roles with the Leadership teams role to lead the organisation in realising the Vision. Once they accepted the difference they settled on four KRAs for the first six months as follows:

- Staff development
- Communications
- Stock Management
- Achieving a National Health & Safety accreditation top mark

Remember, you do not want a long list. At most you only need three or four KRAs, such as the ones listed in the earlier section. We are not looking for business-as-usual goals here.

What you absolutely do not want is for people to think of it in terms of their own roles. There is little point in the marketing director identifying 'marketing' as a KRA, and the new business director declaring, well, 'new business' as another one. People have to be encouraged to think more widely than their own silos.

What is it the *whole team* has to achieve, together, in order to realise the vision?

Stage three – breaking down the key result areas into monthly goals

The team now needs to produce annual or six monthly goals for each of the KRAs agreed in stage two. There may be more than one annual goal for each KRA.

They should take each one in turn and do the following:

- Create milestones (where they should be at the end of three months) for the first quarter for each of the annual goals.
- Decide what needs to be accomplished in month one, in order to move forward
- Debate what would happen if it were possible that the team exceeded expectations in month one.

It is only by having goals for a month at a time that the team will be able to keep the plan moving forward (after all – in the real world no plan survives first contact with the enemy).

The aim is not to get a book of highly prescriptive steps, one and a half inches thick. But, you do want measurable, smart, activities which will lead the team to the goal.

Thus, to return to the example of ABC Construction and its aim to innovate into the areas of wind farms, the plan for month one would look something like this:

- Identify and draw up a list of all the wind farm manufacturers currently working in the UK
- Identify and draw up a list of all the companies that currently supply these wind farm manufacturers. Research their products and methods.
- Find out about the technical specifications of the concrete used for the base of turbines.
- Break down how that differs from ABC Construction's current specifications.
- Explore the issues concerning the delivery of concrete to potentially inhospitable sites.

Now the team has agreed the plan, it is time to go off and make it happen.

Naming a process champion

A high performing team has to have a process owner. His or her role is to nurture each KRA and develop it within the team, as well as being ultimately responsible for procuring all the necessary resources from time to hardware.

This will involve;

- Regularly updating the team on changes or activities that may impact the team's workload, performance or time-frame.
- Coaching team members and encouraging high performance team behaviour
- Explaining the team's vision to outside organisations.
- Measuring the process performance and rewarding the team.

The process champion does not necessarily have to be chosen because of his or her direct connection with the key result area. Just because someone is in R&D, doesn't automatically make them the ideal process champion for innovation.

What is most important is that the person who takes up the challenge of being a process champion is ready to stir things up and keep them on the agenda.

The selection of the process owner should be done by the team themselves on the basis that one chosen by the team will make progress much faster than one arbitrarily assigned from on high. He or she will start off with a special relationship with the team that would take some time for an assigned process owner to achieve.

But – and this is an important but – just because there is a process champion does not mean that everyone needn't worry too much about the plan. They should. After all, if you are working in the shop and no one is coming in through the door, you should care, even if you only work behind the counter.

The process owner is simply there to coordinate the activities between all the people on the team which are supporting a single process. They keep the team focussed and prevent conflicts and distractions. They are not there to make it all happen single-handedly.

The role of the process champion begins once the KRAs have been agreed and the first stages of the month-by-month plan are in place. From then on it is up to him or her to maintain the momentum.

To return once more to ABC Construction, this would mean that, over the next month, after the team has returned to base, the process owner would seek regular updates on the steps agreed above.

Colleagues on the team will be able to tell him or her;

- Details of the competition
- All the current and planned wind farm sites in the country
- The contracts that are being serviced and those that aren't
- The differences in the technical spec in this new market

By the end of the first month, the process owner should easily be able to surmise whether the team is getting the answers to the questions that they want. If, for any reason, there is slippage in the schedule, it is his or her responsibility to find out why.

Maintaining the momentum

At the end of the first month the team should meet again to discuss the progress of the plan.

This meeting, and the regular monthly progress meetings which follow, does not need to be held off site. However, the team leader needs to make it very clear that this meeting is not to be hijacked by day-to-day concerns about something that has gone awry and needs sorting. This process meeting is not business as usual - it is running the business. If people try to use it as a forum to moan about problems with the computer system, or a sales discussion which is going wrong, it is the job of the team leader to refocus everyone on the matter in hand.

This monthly process update is important for a number of reasons:

- No plan, as we all know, survives first contact with the enemy
- As the team fulfils its brief, and returns with fresh information, better approaches will emerge
- Regular discussion of the plan, process and goals will reinforce their importance to the whole team
- It is an opportunity to enjoy viewing appropriate progress and express appreciation
- It is an opportunity to sustain inspiration in support of the vision

It may well be that the team will return and explain that the plan is more difficult to execute than first thought. It may even be proven that the initial plan is unworkable. But, without this process, everything would grind to halt.

Yes, there might be some hitherto unknown barriers for ABC Construction to get into wind farms, but knowing that innovation is the key, the team will have already begun exploring other prospective uses for concrete. Indeed, it is more than likely that, as soon as the team began reporting back its findings over the previous month, the process owner will have already set them off in this direction.

Wind farms, after all, simply came under the heading of innovative new business. It doesn't have to be wind farms. If it is discovered there is a better new market for concrete, all the better. The possibility that discovering an altogether new use may not be what is needed – an already known use which this company is not yet using might be the answer. Yes, innovation can often be staring us in the face.

For a team to come back having achieved 100 per cent of the plan is a rarity. The important thing is they are pursuing the process.

Having a process ensures that the original great ideas get turned into action. It may not be the way that you originally expected, but you will know why and will be light enough on your feet to change course to arrive at your chosen destination in the best way possible.

Time should also be taken in the regular planning meetings to ask the team to score the activities according to the limiting mindsets outlined at the beginning of the exercise.

- On a scale of one to 100, how do they think they are doing now?
- Do they have any evidence to back that up?

Ideally, the score will steadily increase. However, the score is actually less relevant than the regular discussions as to how the team is evolving and meeting its aims and keeping aware of what is important.

The important thing to remember is; unless you re-examine your process on a regular basis, the team, indeed the company, could end up anywhere. Think of it on the basis that; if you don't know why something goes well when it does, you won't be able to repeat it. If everyone is saying; wow, how did you score that goal? Or, how did you do that amazing stroke of a golf club? If you don't know why, you are doomed to ultimate failure because you won't be able to repeat it. But, if you can understand why things happened, you can make them happen again – faster or more frequently.

Process meetings ensure that we do follow up what is critical and important to the team although we have to make sure we don't allow any panics of the moment to divert us from the bigger picture.

If you think of it in sporting terms, the professionals constantly review how they played in every game, what has gone well and what hasn't gone quite so well. They then apply that learning to the next game. OK, not every competitor is going to be the same, but if a team applies that learning and gets into the discipline of examining every competitor, it will inevitably do better on an intellectual, professional and emotional basis.

If you have proper plans and process you won't get to the stage where you are running a multi-million pound business but cancelling your Monday meeting because there is a problem with the marketing programme. In the grand scheme of things, that is incidental to the bigger picture. You want a team that adapts to circumstance and looks forward. Plan and process helps you do that. Plan and process constantly allows the cream to come to the surface and hence all feel good about progress.

How plan and process helps us to reach our goals

A client once said to me; the reason we are making progress with you is because you turn up every month. I had to answer that yes, that was true. But, I added, the really clever thing was that their boss thought it a good idea to engage in this process in the first place, because, without me being there to keep them on the track they chose they won't have done it!

Monthly visibility, whether it is me ensuring a team has the discipline to stick to the plan, or they take on the job and do it themselves, focuses a team on the right stuff. Forget all the petty politicking and pointless little goals which do little but serve the person who is obsessed with getting them done. With process, a team takes the time to concentrate on a small number of goals which really mean something. Every team should be doing this.

Process creates openness, honesty and consistency and helps everyone recognise that they do rely on each other. It provides a forum for positive challenge as well as much needed constructive conflict. It shows everyone is serious about what needs to be done and tackles all those limiting mind-sets. That is part of how to create a high performing team ….. have a Plan and Process to bring it to life.

PRACTICAL GUIDE to PROCESS and PLANNING with your TEAM:

- Processes are a series of activities which have a start point and an end point and spell out the importance of tasks and the time commitment required to complete those tasks

- They define organisational and operational boundaries within which the team is expected to operate.

- It stops in their tracks any energy sapping and time wasting turf wars over what the team should be focussing on.

- Having a Plan as described here and sticking to the process of regularly reviewing it keeps the plan on track and prevents diversions which let individuals off the hook.

- It requires determined leadership to keep it 'on track' and energised.

- Process can and should be challenged, though always within the framework of the long term vision of the future.

- Use your plan as a compass rather than a detailed road map.

- Whilst it is not an easy one, you must identify the limiting mindsets or things just will not change.

- Having the plan and reviewing it regularly with integrity is the only certain way of controlling the results you want.

Chapter three - Attitude

Do you get out of bed flying at a thousand feet, raring for each and every challenge that the next 12 hours can throw at you?

Or, do you brace yourself to shoulder the burden of whatever will hit you that day and dread every moment?

Every day, as we awake, we are gifted with the ability to choose our attitude. We can be upbeat and confident, or gloomy and cowed. Your answers to the two simple questions at the top of this page say everything about you and how you grasp the opportunities presented to you every single day of your life. If you are constantly paralysed by fear of what lies ahead, you won't have any chance of creating and sustaining a high performing team.

It's an old adage, but it is as true as it ever was; if you think you are not up to it, or can't do it, then you are probably absolutely right. So what can you do about feeling in the frame of mind to chose positive expectation over negative expectation? Mindfulness teaches us that concern about the future is merely an illusion and that worry is a negative drain on our energy. The difference between productive thought (leading to productive action) and unproductive thought is 'being present', being in this moment, right now, taking positive steps NOW.

Opportunities are everywhere, but you will only see them if you are alert and looking for them. You may be the type who has a positive outlook and can see the possibility, yet there is frustration because those around you who do not share your perspective. It is a simple law of life that you and they will see and find what your radar is tuned into and looking for. If your head is kept low to protect yourself from potential harm, those opportunities will just pass you by, again and again.

Plus, as if it is not bad enough that you are missing out, you are also setting the tone for your whole business. Fear of change is one of the most corrosive attitudes that can inflict a team.

Psychologists will tell you that attitude is related to self-image and social acceptance.

We all have a profound effect on the people we meet and the teams we work with or lead. It happens on a number of levels both instinctively and subconsciously and if you are downbeat it manifests itself in a myriad of ways, from the way you convey your negative thoughts and feelings, through to your slumped and beaten body language. If you are not confident, other people sense your aura and will be adversely affected by your insecurities, self-doubt and confusion. If you haven't got the right attitude, people will still automatically empathise with you and try to adopt a similar hangdog, or defeated position. Would you be proud to lead a team like that? Of course not.

Transforming that fear into a flexible, open attitude is the only way to succeed in a world that will not slow down for you, however much you want it to. Attitude is a vital principle of high performing teams, because if you can get the whole team to take the same positive position as you, then you are flying. This is a critical ingredient in the ever changing mix that sustains a high performing Team.

One team I worked with, a failing subsidiary of a global organisation which had not made a profit in over a decade, had taken on a tough Scotsman as chief executive in a last ditch attempt to stem the losses. I think both he and I, indeed probably the whole team, knew that if the market conditions had been better, the subsidiary would have been sold off many years before. Somehow, my Scottish leader had to find a way to stabilise the situation, stop the firm haemorrhaging cash and even find a way to show a small profit! Plus, all the while, the entire team would be fearing for their jobs and expecting the parent company to just throw in the towel once and for all to cut their already enormous losses.

If ever there was a circumstance that needed a positive 'attitude', this was it. This, as we proved, (and I will talk about how later in this chapter) was the key to turning this dog's dinner of a company around. It is impossible to get the best out of everyone without the best possible pragmatic attitude.

We need a positive attitude because:

Negative people will usually tell you that they are not negative, they are just being realistic. This is utter rubbish. What they are actually doing is locking themselves into a negative world of their own creation and I will tell you why. All for one and one for all Teamwork requires a proactive positive attitude of being there for each other. The high performing Team isn't a bundle of false fun, it does, however chose to be offering support and sincere interest in each other.

If someone thinks negatively, their subconscious mind will constantly seek out confirmation that the world is indeed a terrible place where nothing goes right. Guess what? That is exactly what they see. Then, because they are constantly expecting negative results, they never take any risks or try anything remotely daring and amazingly the world remains a dismal place where nothing goes right.

Imagine though, if you allowed your subconscious mind to think positively. If you *expect* positive results and things to turn out well, hey presto, they do. Once you move past the fear that things can't be done, it is amazing what starts happening. The only difference between positive thinkers and the negative folk is the positive ones changed their attitude to see opportunities from a different perspective.

The great thing about getting the right attitude in a high performing team is it blows selfish motivations out of the water. Instead of thinking how this initiative or that may affect them, or how much more work it is going to heap on their shoulders, they'll view every move in terms of what is best for the team as a whole.

Imagine if the boss says; we need to process these orders faster, because we are working at 60 per cent capacity and it needs to be more like 80 per cent. Most times, the manager of the department responsible for the processing will react with dismay when he or she hears the ominous news at a meeting. They will dread having to go back and break the news to their team and may even try their utmost to wheedle out of it then and there.

But how would a member of a positive thinking, high performing team react? They'll open up and realise this is a great move for customers. OK, right now, they can only think of ideas to make the process work at 65 per cent capacity, but once they get together with their people, who knows what they could work out? Why leave it at 80 per cent they may say – let's try for 100 per cent! If they work together, the sky is the limit.

The great thing about attitude is it does work just like this. It breeds more confidence. If a team is positive, no one is nervous about saying, wow, I'm not sure how we're going to beat 65 per cent capacity, because in the next breath you know they are going to be brimming with ideas of how to darn well try.

Demonstrating worry and concern is not a signal they are not up to the job, it is merely a signal that they are striving to get the best result.

Having a great attitude even has an impact on your metabolism. If someone is feeling positive then they are automatically more energetic and light-hearted. They can accept and take on work that might seem stressful to someone who is in a negative state. Which of these two teams would you like to be a part of? A winning attitude gets a thumbs up from me every time. If nothing else, I just can't wait to see what they can achieve.

Attitude is not about....

- Putting on a brave face and repeating the mantra that everything will probably work out OK in the long run.
- Finding a way to see problems in a new light. In fact, with a proper positive attitude, you won't even see problems as problems at all.

Attitude is nothing to do with having a so-called Positive Mental Attitude (PMA). PMA is a catch-all expression which generally means very little. Underneath the gloss, no one really believes in PMA. It's all smiles and high fives, but there is no substance to it and it is not deep-rooted. It is all on the outside. It is not enough to *say* you have PMA. You have to take action too and that comes from truly believing that your object of desire is obtainable.

My Scottish leader went well beyond PMA – he became a promoter and challenger. He promoted the inspiring vision of the future daily and he challenged every negative suggestion, decision or thought. He encouraged all the people involved to take the vision into account and make the effort to see the positive possibilities of the situation in front of them. It wasn't too long before his immediate team latched onto the idea that the glass is half full, rather than half empty. This quickly started to cascade throughout the whole workforce. That is how he managed to turn the subsidiary around.

What he did was real though. He didn't just talk the talk – he genuinely believed what he was saying. Anything else would have been a waste of everyone's time.

Think about it another way. Imagine a team get together before a big match. According to PMA folklore, the key to getting everyone focussed on the task ahead is to get into a huddle to listen to the captain say how well they are going to play. We're going to lick the opposition, he'll yell, displaying his textbook PMA. Do you think they will? Well, I guarantee that if they do it will be nothing to do with the faux motivational huddle, because by the time each member of the team has turned around and pumped their legs to warm themselves up they'll have forgotten every single word from the captain. Individuals will find their minds clouded with thoughts such as; what will happen if the ball lands on my head? Will Bill get into the right position this time, or will he ruin all my hard work setting up that shot, just like last time? Everyone, to a man (or woman) will go straight into self-centred mode.

Without a genuine can do mindset, it is all just words.

Attitude is not just an upbeat exterior. It is how you feel about yourself. I mean how you *really* feel about yourself.

When you ask someone about their attitude, you will invariably get a dubious response designed to preserve a positive self-image. It is human nature that most people who are asked how things are going, say; everything is great. Part of this is because we are all socially conditioned not to go into a monologue about how our life stinks, our roof is leaking, we've had a cold for the whole winter and the conflict at home is unbearable. However, the real crux of the reason is; they are just saying that because attitudinally we all want others to see us as a success.

You only have to look at Facebook for the stream of ' look at what a wonderful time I am having' pictures of smiles and glasses raised' by people you often know to be truly unhappy or even depressed! We have been conditioned, or our egos have conditioned us to respond that all is well. This is not the positive attitude I am referring to here. The trouble is, it stands out a mile when it just isn't true.

I know the score. For a big chunk of my life I was a salesman and in a pressurised, commission-led environment like that you are almost forced into being outwardly upbeat. Unfortunately, unless you actually feel it and have consciously thought about where you are going and believe in what you are trying to do, it will be false. You'll know it, your prospects will know it and your whole team will too.

To create the environment for high performing teams, the team leader has to be in control of the best possible attitude. If you do that you will be a suitable coach and role model for the team, as well as any other teams you come in contact with. A positive attitude is infectious!

Attitude is….

- An honest, clear sense of purpose, which cannot help but create a world around you where *everyone* is growing and benefiting to their maximum true potential.
- An understanding that we are surrounded by a world of possibilities where dreams can and do become a reality.
- Being favourably disposed to change instead of constantly fearing it and hiding away from it.
- The way to be appropriately decisive, rather than just talking the talk.

A powerful, empowering attitude that is open to challenge and overcoming constraints, means that when problems come along, a high performing team is not fazed for a second. They simply start thinking about how they are going to deal with the hurdle quickly and effectively. They don't for one moment stop to think, why is this happening on my watch? How am I supposed to deal with this? I wonder if I can palm this off on another department.

With great attitude, people take the knocks on the chin and then look for a proactive way to make something work and turn the situation on its head. A problem is no longer a problem, it is an opportunity.

Most teams want to conform socially. People want to *act* like everyone else, because it means they don't have to think too deeply about why or what they are doing. They are content for everything to just tick over because social conformity means not stepping away from the norm and not speaking out or saying what is really on your mind. It is like the old army expression; they've got their thumbs up their bums and their minds in neutral! Of course, for a high performing team, you want exactly the opposite.

High performing teams are made up of individuals who want to be high performing within the team. It won't ever be a high performing team if people don't feel able to say what is on their minds. By creating a positive, can do, atmosphere, the team leader will have an environment where everyone feels safe to say what they think. They will feel free to challenge one another without the person who is being challenged sulking because they feel singled out, or because someone is having a pop at them. Team members will even feel empowered enough to challenge the team leader, rather than keeping quiet when they think the person at the top has clearly missed the point. That's great. As soon as people say, hey boss, I think that is a bad idea, why don't we do this instead, you're halfway there. Once people are willing to disrupt the normal thought patterns, that is when things really start to happen. It means the team is thinking about winning this thing, not keeping their heads down and limping through to the end of the day.

This is where it starts. It then transfers to enjoying a passion for powerful RESULTS.

The leader finds the right attitude first…

Our Scottish leader definitely got it right and the story had a very happy ending – the leadership team led the organisation into profit for the first time within twelve months! It would not have been possible to create this high performing team without the 'attitude' ingredient. And, that in great part was down to him.

Attitude is a key component of a high performing team, but it never 'just happens'. It always starts from the top with the team leader becoming the attitude role model. If the person at the top of a team won't, or can't, get their attitude in the right place, then they have no right to expect a better performance from the ranks below.

Once the man or woman at the top has their own attitude sorted, they can start taking their decisions in line with the vision of the business. That is when the magic begins. The team below will see that their leader's demeanour is now a core part of them, not just an external act. It is who they are, what they stand for, how they operate and how they make their decisions. Nothing is based on superficial acts to make everyone think that the leader is good bloke, or just to show they are good at making decisions.

If the attitude at the top isn't good, it stands out a mile, as I found with another CEO who briefed me to work with his team. He had a highly competent group on an individual-by-individual basis, he was clear about what he wanted and knew he could rely on the team's all pervasive 'bottom line' culture to deliver the figures. However, when I met everyone on the team individually, it was obvious that the CEO was not very visible to his immediate team. At the same time, thanks to shareholder issues which constantly distracted the CEO, he was not always the most patient listener in his own team meetings. It was not that he did have a bad, or even negative attitude, yet his behaviour did not present a positive role model which would lead to everyone focussing on operating as a cohesive team. No one could accuse the CEO of being negative, however, he was not available to display positive encouragement; the ingredient was missing and so was the performance as a team.

The first and important step in getting the right attitude begins with a leader finding and understanding a clear sense of *purpose*. If you are surrounded by a negative, fearful team it is because you yourself have not defined and demonstrated your positive purpose. You are demanding better results, but have not gone into the bigger picture of where you are now and where you want to be in the future. To your 'observers' your purpose appears as though it is ' profit at all cost' and whilst that is critical, it probably is not your personal purpose.!

So, if you want the right attitude, first find your purpose.

Finding your purpose

The best part of purpose is; it is not all about achievement, or a huge promotion, or a massive salary raise. Purpose is not a list of goals. Purpose is something that everyone can express continually in order to bring them pleasure.

Screenwriter Leo Roston said about the subject "I cannot believe that the purpose of life is to be happy. I think that the purpose of life is to be useful, to be responsible, to be compassionate. It is above all to matter, to count, to stand for something to have made a difference that you lived at all" – wow.

To find your purpose, take this simple test.

Write down your answers to the following questions:

- What do you like about yourself?

- How do you most like spending your time?
- What do you imagine is a perfect world for you?
- Answer this question in 60 seconds "what should I do with my life from now on?" ask it now, no matter what age or experience you have to date.

Answer honestly. Quite often, people have never bothered to question why they get out of bed in the morning, or whether they even like what they are doing every day. Most of the time they have given it no more thought than the fact that they are doing it to pay their mortgage, or because it is the job they have got. After leaving full-time education they just get swept along in the normal cycle of life, where you get a job, get a house and car and then think about getting a better paid job, a bigger house and a faster car.

Most professional people don't have trouble getting out of bed, but are they seriously motivated? Have they evolved a genuine passion for what they are doing, or is it just a well-paid job? To define your purpose, you need to get clarity and to do this you need to think about your motivations more clearly.

Now review your answers to these questions and identify what links these answers together and define ways you can use your favourite characteristics, abilities and attitudes in activities you like best to manifest your new found vision of a perfect world.

This is your true life purpose.

When you have your purpose the best possible attitude is now going to emerge. Your positive thinking in support of your purpose is a mental attitude that will admit into your mind thoughts, words and images that are conducive to growth, expansion and success. It is a mental attitude that expects good and favourable results. A positive mind anticipates happiness, joy, health and a successful outcome of every situation and action. Whatever the mind expects, it finds.

Humans are motivated to maintain consistency between beliefs, attitudes and behaviours.

Once a leader has the answers to the questions above, they will begin to be clearer about their purpose and this, in turn, will guide them to a greater clarity around their beliefs and values. If these are aligned, a true 'attitude' will emerge and they will naturally be the model for your team and those around them. Then, and only then, can the leader of a high performing team take on the responsibility for helping others discover their productive life purpose.

Here are some rules I learnt somewhere along my journey:

- Everything happens for a reason and a purpose and it does serve me.
- There is no such thing as failure.
- Whatever happens, take responsibility.
- It's not necessary to understand everything to be able to use everything.
- People are your greatest resource.
- Work is play.
- There is no abiding success without commitment.

Motivational speakers and sports coaches will tell you time and time again to "keep your heart in the oven and your head in the fridge". It is your heart that has the passion and I challenge everyone to truly know their passion without first being connected to a real life purpose. As to keeping your head in the fridge, having plans, goals performance coaching, discipline and systems need to be a part of how you manifest to the world what you want. Naturally, an important part of what you want is, of course, a high performing team.

….Then apply that attitude to the team

Most teams don't just automatically acquire great attitudes. What makes things even more complicated though, is the fact that they don't even begin with *the same* attitudes, great or otherwise. It is generally the norm that, even if they are pretty smart and hardworking, everyone on the team will have strong individual attitudes. Some will be pulling this way; others will be pulling away in another direction. No one much cares what everyone else gets up to.

The beauty of a leader coming in with a strong purpose and positive attitude, is it will become easier for everyone to understand and align behind his or her thinking. Once you start getting alignment (and we will discuss alignment in more detail in the next chapter) you are on the way to getting a very high performing team indeed.

So, as soon as the person at the top has discovered their purpose, they can begin to coach and encourage the rest of the team. They should make their beliefs and values apparent in everything they do, from the environment they create around them, to their more open and healthy attitude.

There is no need for any bullshit, no need for any high fives and absolutely no need for any soon-to-be-ignored team huddles. The team will see that attitude, understand that purpose and will have something to get behind. The place for the 'huddle' is to remind that 'we are in this together', not alone in a silo.

Teams need purpose. Otherwise they'll say (or think) 'what will be will be' or 'I just take things as they come'. That doesn't sound very inspiring to anyone and it is not a sign of a group of people who are pushing the envelope in their eagerness to get things done. In fact, these statements are excuses masquerading as no real purpose at all.

Imagine then, the effect of a conscious articulated purpose. Once you get a high performing team, where everyone has a purpose and a positive attitude, it doesn't matter if they have a bad day personally or a set back at the office. These things happen and things will always try to throw us off course. The point is, if you have been through the process and have defined that purpose and got the team to buy into the positive attitude, having a bad day will make no difference whatsoever to your long term goals. You and your team will take it in their stride. Having a positive mindset, means everyone is more than likely to take any set back in a pragmatic and realistic way. OK, we didn't get that tender, but there will be another along soon. What a shame that new product didn't take off, but never mind, we have another 12 coming through in its place. It doesn't change why you decided to go and do what you are trying to do in the first place.

Recruit for attitude – and deal with the internal terrorists

You can, of course, heighten the odds of getting a high performing team by making sure you recruit the right sort of people who are already predisposed to positive thinking. If you ask the right sort of behavioural questions at the interview stage, it is possible to quickly spot the positive ones. If you ask someone how they felt about their last employer and they quickly launch into a diatribe about what a loser their former boss was, the alarm bells should ring. A good trick is to probe into how they responded to an awkward change in the past. If they reply with relish and tell you how they rose to the occasion and loved the challenge, it is a great sign. Alternatively, if they tell you what a hash their teammates made of it all, it does not bode well. By getting prospective candidates to describe a real situation, you will quickly get a real measure of their personality.

We don't all get the opportunity to start with a clean slate though. Most of the time, we have to make do with what we have got. Unfortunately, it is a sad fact of modern business life that there will always be some people who don't believe and indeed will never ever believe. These sorts of people will put up an invisible barrier against all forms of positive thought. Their words will tell you everything is great, but their attitude and demeanour will show you that it is anything but great.

Whilst we will be covering the enormous impact of ego on Teams later on, it is right to acknowledge here , why often very talented individuals have so much negative energy . Their current 'Senior Role' is often a significant part of their personal identity, and the ego wants desperately for it to be perfect – any hint of a blemish causes them to feel under attack ! Hence the negative and defensive attitude.

Generally, most teams will break down into one of three groups. The first will be instantly excited, enthused and inspired by the positive example from the top. The second may be a little slow to climb on board and may even need some encouragement and mentoring, but they will gradually bear fruit. The third group, which I call internal terrorists, resolutely refuse to follow the leader, change their negative attitude and be inspired to follow the vision.

These internal terrorists invariably make it their life's work to snipe from the side-lines and do their best to infect their colleagues with their negativity. Fortunately I find these to be in the minority these days but not completely absent. Clearly, if you are building a high performing team you would like most of its members from the first group. However, with your new positive and can do attitude, you will be inspired by the challenge of inspiring the team members from the second group.

Those in the third group however, the internal terrorists, deserve some thorough examination because you have to decide what to do about them.

The bad news is, most of these internal terrorists are plausible and not easy to spot. Indeed, even if team leaders do feel uneasy about someone, most find it easy to ignore them because they don't want to think too deeply about why this person or that is not performing. Until something happens.

I once worked with a team at a motor insurance company and it was not until the third time that I met with the team that I began to sense something was very wrong. We were conducting an exercise where everyone was asked to say one thing they liked about other members of the team, one thing they'd like someone to do less of and one thing they particularly admired. I couldn't put my finger on it, but something seemed terribly amiss. None of the answers seemed to add up to a full picture. The next time I saw the company, one of the members of the team was no longer there. I asked what had happened and was told that attitudinally they did not fit. The exercises I had been doing with the firm had shown up just how a disruptive force that person had become. Working together as a team had lifted their level of understanding.

It turned out that this person, who was responsible for a very large number of people who were administering an important part of the business, was spending a large amount of her time warmly befriending subordinates, while at the same time telling other people in the firm that various members of the team were actually not very good. For a long while this was the 'truth' in that firm and it was very damaging indeed. It was not just damaging to those who had their careers blighted by the team leaders sniping, but also to the morale of the entire organisation.

I am often asked my opinion as to what I would do in a situation like this. Should a company immediately part company with their internal terrorist? Or can they be changed and brought into line with everyone else?

In my experience, more than 20 per cent of people can, and do, change their attitude. But that leaves 80 per cent who never will, whatever you do. Eckhart Tolle refers to our ability to create illusions in our own minds about the past – he refers to them as a 'Pain Body' and those 80% are allowing their Pain Body to be their manufactured truth. In this case, there is no alternative and they have to go because otherwise they will be a very powerful negative force.

Of those that appear to be able to change, it is worthwhile providing some focus support, or one on one mentoring in order to help them fit in the environment in which they are working and think about things differently. This will entail persuading this person to be open and honest while you ask them if they would like to come with you on this journey. Ask them straight out; what is the biggest thing standing in your way of you operating in this way? Then you need to listen, really listen, to their replies. You need to use active listening to regurgitate what they are saying because what you are trying to achieve is to get this person to solve this problem themselves.

If they can be helped to see things differently, then the door is open to change.

Either way though, a leader of a business harbouring an internal terrorist, needs to make their mind up about how to deal with it. And fast.

Don't ever be tempted to just cut internal terrorists out of the loop though. You are trying to create a high performing team. To just cut someone out of the game is like not giving the ball to your scrum half because you don't trust them. It is totally self-defeating. You may as well not play them in the team at all. Address the problem. Either get rid of them or infect them with the positive attitude.

Always act on your instincts and use your intuition to ask better questions. If you are just not sure about someone, use your vision for the future and purpose as the springboard to question their ability, credibility and confidence. Don't ever be frightened to ask more pertinent questions when your intuition is saying something is wrong. Even if you can't put your finger on it, don't wait until something bad happens, use that intuition to go and find the internal terrorist. Then deal with them.

How attitude helps us to reach our goals

How many people ever really stop to consider the true possibilities of their position and opportunities right now? As we have seen here, it is very easy to get swept along in what we do, enjoy the trappings of our hard work and success, yet give our actual purpose no real consideration.

I saw a classic example of this with a long-standing team leader who I have coached personally and also worked with his various teams as he progressed up the career ladder. His most recent move was into a high profile new job as managing director of a subsidiary of a prestigious global firm. Such was the seniority of the role that he was asked to take a lengthy period of gardening leave before he could take up the job.

This chap is your typically glass half full character and threw himself into his gardening leave with the energy and fervour which he has used in all of his 'day' jobs. He dissected the period into three parts, beginning with a burst of domestic chores, followed by a longer and better family holiday than was usual and ended it with a spell of research and preparation for the taxing task ahead.

What was missing from this admirable period of preparation? He never once took the time to consider his purpose. There was no argument that it was a great job, but he did not consider why *he* was doing it. He had no clarity about his motives for doing it, no sense of purpose and consequently was starting with completely the wrong attitude.

As his long-term coach, this is something I addressed straight away, starting with an exercise to explore why he really got out of bed in the mornings. Laudably his purpose now is to be making a measureable difference 'fast'.

His response to finding his purpose at long last? Wow, he said, that is different, now I can really motor. And, I am pleased to say, now he is indeed really motoring, making a difference in both long and short term with the team and the bottom line results.

PRACTICAL GUIDE to LEVERAGING on ATTITUDE to IMPACT TEAM PERFORMANCE:

- Clarify your own Purpose and Vision first – that will fuel you.
- Your attitude is all about how you grasp the opportunities presented to you
- If you are constantly paralysed by fear of what lies ahead, you won't have any chance of creating and sustaining a high performing team.
- Attitude begins at the top and flows down through the team
- To find your attitude, you must first discover your purpose
- Attitude is a choice you make
- As a role model, in all areas of your life, attitude will impact others more than anything else.
- Utilise your Corporate or Team Vision and look for ways of relating it to your daily challenges.
- Create a practice of DAILY writing down what you appreciated (everything from the weather to the corporate victory) about the day before. (This causes you to carry the good vibrations rather than the bad ones into today).
- Request of people that they bring constructive solutions to meetings alongside the issues or problem.

Chapter four - Alignment

Imagine a boat. Scattered around the edges of this boat are six individuals and each of them has a paddle. They are told that they need to get to the nearest island, or they will not survive the day. However, they are not allowed to communicate with their fellow rowers. Not one word.

What do you think will happen?

Chances are the boat will pretty soon be going round and round in circles as everyone heads off doggedly in a different direction and chaos will ensue. Certainly it will not be a smooth journey.

This is not unlike most companies that I have seen. There will always be some members of the team who resolutely stick to the same strategy they've followed since the day they joined. They will paddle along in that direction, come what may – sticking with their individual strengths as one of the ancient philosophers once stated "it is impossible that which one thinks one already knows"!

Unfortunately, as other recruits come on board they will probably stick loyally to whatever strategy was in place when they signed-up, thus perpetuating no change / improvement. So, clearly there will be another group of people paddling in a multitude of directions.

Then, there will be others who think they know better and decide to follow their own plan motivated by playing to their own strengths and experience.

There will also inevitably be the odd one (our old friend the internal terrorist) who deliberately tries to stick a spanner in the works, just for the sake of it, by carousing off in their own sweet way, exhausted due to hard work apparently not advancing us to our chosen destination.

So, as the corporate ship metaphorically goes around in circles, what do you do? The knee jerk reaction in most teams is to blame someone, anyone. The human resources director might blame sales for paddling off in the wrong way, while the marketing director may point the finger firmly in the direction of the 'disorganised' techies. The sales division will mutter darkly about the accounts department and so on.

Misaligned Teams are subtly ineffective, not because of any intentional behaviour but due to the unconscious damaging intent of continuing to play to past strengths and experience.

Sadly, they will all be missing the point. The truth is, there is no possibility of creating a high performing team unless everyone is aligned and rowing in the same direction. It might sound totally obvious, but the truth is not lessened in the telling of it: you all have to pull together in the same direction if you want to get anywhere. A misaligned team rapidly loses power and momentum – as mentioned earlier, misalignment usually happens unconsciously yet it is a debilitating dysfunction in Teams.

Figure 4: 'You don't have to agree but you do have to align'

To cap it all, unless something is done, the leader just gets frustrated from his vantage point at the front of the boat as he or she watches the chaos of everyone pulling in different directions. Pretty soon the situation is self-perpetuating because no one is doing anything to solve the problem.

If a team is aligned, communicates freely and understand how to make things happen, they will work together to overcome any barriers to getting things done.

It is up to the team leader to give everyone a shared purpose and direction. He or she has to keep everyone aligned to the company goals. That is when you really start motoring towards your goal.

We need alignment because

- If a team is aligned, individuals on that team will be able to collaborate effectively and overcome any conflicts.
- It will help individuals overcome any false or hidden assumptions about what the company is trying to do.
- It will unite everyone to become focussed on the common values, strategic priorities and purpose of the team.
- It will help everyone develop the mindset and capability to be able to achieve those strategic priorities.
- It will create momentum and with it a satisfying environment.
- Fundamentally it ensures that 'I' wins because the 'Team' wins first.

In short – teamwork works and it creates an enjoyable environment. Oh, and incidentally, that word 'joy' crops up again and again when you meet winning teams.

If a team works together the whole is infinitely more powerful than the sum of the parts. Contrary to what we were all taught at school, one plus one can actually equal three, four or even more – it usually requires some ego management and development of personal emotional self awareness as well as impulse control. (These are recognised characteristics of quality of Emotional Intelligence Dr Reuven Bar – On.)

If you are still not convinced, here is a compelling financial argument:

According to official research, aligning your team's talent to new roles and challenges equates to increased productivity, with 58 per cent of professionals saying that they were interested in doing more.[1] That's quite a leap. Honest appraisal of past experiences may offer you further evidence of frustrating times relating to unsatisfactory progress from Teams full of talented people.

Get your team all pulling in the same direction and you can virtually guarantee improved performance, productivity and results. It is also less stressful for everyone concerned because they will see that, at long last, the boat is no longer spinning around in circles and making them feel dizzy. They can immediately witness that the fruits of their efforts are helping the vessel move steadily forward to get everyone to their goal. Not only are they a vital part of the operation, but nobody's efforts are being wasted. Who wouldn't like to climb on board a boat like that?

---

[1] Accenture: Untapped Potential: Stretching Toward the Future 2009

The logic really does stack up but in my experience what happens in the real world is very different. When I meet teams for the first time they typically think they are almost aligned, but their behaviours indicate that this is far from the truth. A case in point would be a team I have worked with in recent months which is peripatetic but just doesn't seem to know it. There clearly needs to be a very high level of interdependency and interconnectivity in order for this company to succeed.

When I probed further to see how they ended up all heading off in different directions, I was told that the team typically only meets once a month and the agenda is invariably a very busy one. Indeed, one of them described the meetings as a 'down in the trenches, exhausting, day where we never seem to get everything covered'.

Their 'busy' meetings are taken up dealing with the mechanics rather than the relationships in the team and as a result everyone is heading off in slightly different directions. They like many senior Leaders I meet tend to glamorise busy-ness! The team's orientation has been very task orientated which is all about achieving the mission and goals. However, relationship orientation, which is much more about cultivating relationships that have synergy, have been largely forgotten. Yet, a team needs to be task *and* relationship orientated in order to function with integrity and be aligned towards producing added-value outcomes. An example of their mis-aligned approach was the word 'best' appeared in their Vision and Mission statements but each member had very different definitions of what 'best' meant in all areas of the organisation.

The solution to this problem was to adjust their monthly meetings to include 'team development'. This has greatly contributed to an improved harmonious environment where give and take is easy. By shifting away from criticising condemning and complaining to attitudes of appreciation and application (doing rather than just talking about it) and practice ,in a short space of time, alignment is beginning to be the natural course for this once fractured team and enhanced proactive communication is taking place between meetings obviating much of the 'issue discussion time'.

Alignment frees up your team – and your future

All businesses work in cycles that are rather similar to life. To be blunt; they are created, they grow and then they die. Their longevity is just as unpredictable as that for human life, in that some businesses go on steadily for decades and others appear, are an overnight success and then sink without trace with equal speed. It is the task of an able and intuitive leader to spot a business in decline and concurrently begin a new business or division to eventually supersede the original venture. They then have to successfully manage the smooth transition and plan ahead how to evolve the organization.

What has this got to do with alignment, you may ask? Well, everything. If the team leader cannot communicate that the team has to work together for what is happening today *and* for what is happening tomorrow, then all will be lost.

Many years ago, in my former career, I was promoted to sales director. After grafting so hard for so long as a regional sales manager I was delighted with my big break. At last, I thought, I can run this show the way I want to. I was like a kid with a new train set. Then, my perceptive CEO reminded me that, in actual fact, it was my company's train set. They made it quite clear that they expected me to play a key role in planning for the future, not just making sure I hit my targets in my own sweet way today.

Imagine how I felt. Apart from anything else, sales is a discipline which is particularly vulnerable to what is going on in the here and now. If I had a good year, I would make my target and get my bonus. What did I care what happened next year, or the year after that? It was not my problem that the R&D department was coming up with products that no one wanted, or that marketing was producing old fashioned, badly received campaigns. I was doing just fine, thank you very much.

What I didn't understand when I commenced that role, but do now, is that my single-minded strategy was actually contributing to depleting the energy of the whole of the executive team! While everyone was busy thinking of their own roles, we were all pulling in different directions and the whole company was losing momentum. I was paddling hard, 'where was everyone else' was my limiting contribution! If I had stopped to consider the team as a whole, we could have worked together to achieve our individual goals. Then, I wouldn't just achieve my targets for the year, we would all be helping the company (and each other) towards a brighter future. Oh how I wish I had understood 'alignment' back then.

How could this all have been different? Simple. If my CEO had successfully communicated to me that it was my responsibility to deliver for today and tomorrow too, I could have been made to realize that being aligned with my colleagues would actually give me more time to reach my goals, not less, I would have seen the point in delivering – Marketing would have been more supportive and so on.

Team leaders have a big motivational task here, which, when working well, will release focused energy towards the desired direction. There is a deep need to have everyone synchronized with what is best for the team. Everyone needs to be in sync with what is desirable rather than not desirable. The team needs to be working towards new possibilities rather than against them.

I won't kid you. It will hurt, the team I discussed above, who I have been working with recently, had to face some tough and personal feedback before they started to have a relationship orientation to their teamwork. It is always a strain for everyone learning to do something different. Once you learn to work as a team though, the turbo kicks in and you will all get there faster with less strain AND more enjoyable.

Alignment is...

- Finding a proper structural framework
- Promoting a genuine culture of understanding and trust
- Fostering communication skills which concentrate on the production of extraordinary relationships
- The harmonious way to delivering the results you want
- Being comfortable whilst being vulnerable with each other

Let's play a game. Imagine yourself as a member of a team. You are in a meeting with the team leader and he (or she) is letting off steam about something that has gone very wrong. Now, this something is not really anything to do with your area of responsibility. So what do you do?

- Chip in and say, yes, that department screwed something up for me last month too?
- Keep very quiet, stare into space and be very grateful that it is not you in the firing line this time?

If you are not part of a high performing team, I'd put money on the fact that you're probably going to go for the second answer. Most teams have developed a courteous agreement between themselves, a form of passive compliance, where dissent is not obvious and everyone keeps to them selves. Passionate dialogue around issues and opportunities only happens when someone feels under attack. Sound familiar?

As anyone in a senior role will attest, trying to accomplish complex tasks in an atmosphere rife with high levels of interruption, confrontation and emotion about proposed courses of action, is not easy. Most colleagues don't want to 'do' each other's jobs, but they usually have a strong view on the best way to go about things outside their own particular sphere. Unfortunately this view is not always positive and they'll never do their colleagues the courtesy of confronting them to their face. Meanwhile, these same people are equally forthright in zealously guarding against anything that might encroach upon, or negatively affect, their area of responsibility.

What it all adds up to is an atmosphere of suspicion and self-preservation, which is so insular that it is not at all conducive to getting anyone to collaborate or cooperate. Sadly, this lack of challenge of either their own role, or that of others, means that everyone in a team is often content with a mediocre performance.

The result? No one can get close to delivering 100 per cent on their promises.

Much of this is driven by fear. Fear of the unknown, fear that one individual may be exposed by another's incompetence or excellence, fear of accountability and fear of getting it wrong.

This fear heightens the tension among everyone on the team and distracts them from the task in hand. It stops anyone, indeed everyone, from stepping up to the plate and doing anything creative. I speak from personal experience as a culprit as well as observations of now hundreds of Leadership Teams; too frequently individuals are too invested in their own specialness. Our ego often tells us that we are much better than we really are. It also encourages people to keep their heads down in their own little silos in the hope that no one notices them.

Imagine though, if that fear disappeared. Imagine if there was a way to:

- Increase collaboration, feedback and management of differences
- Encourage the team to give honest 360 degree feedback on all the areas that really need attention – even if it is their own
- Find a mutual agreement on roles and responsibilities – where everyone is prepared to muck in when needed, even if it is not 'their job'.
- Foster an atmosphere of mutual accountability.
- Abolish those silos forever!
- Enjoy personal regard in a balanced way with everyone on the Team

Alignment can make all of these things happen and more. It will create a climate of understanding which will lead to trust. Fear will be pushed into the background when the true spirit of the team is allowed to flourish.

Every member of a properly aligned, high performing, team will agree to the direction the company is going in and the value of individual roles on that team. They will also have complete clarity on how it will all get done. Everyone on the team will also have a personal commitment where each person trusts each other and is honest in their expectations. What this all adds up to is a climate of high challenge and support. To encourage this climate will be to contribute to a culture which says this as a great team to be a part of – a place where challenge as well as professional vocational satisfaction are high.

Alignment is never done

Right ho, you may think, this alignment lark sounds pretty important and effective when we get it right. I had better get on to it. A quick search on Google will find you a whole bunch of organisations that run alignment workshops and off you will go. That's great as far as it goes. The problem is; alignment is not something you do in a day, tick the box and move on in relief that that is that part of team-building sorted. Alignment is never done. It is never finished. It is leadership's role to keep it on course. Constantly.

Why? Well, with a bit of encouragement and a loud hailer, you may well be able to get your team rowing in enough unity to scrabble to one side. The problem is, as soon as you walk away with your megaphone and get on with something else, the chances are everyone will resume their original mind set and all start pulling in different directions again – not intentionally, that is the way our ego connives to drive us without our conscious efforts to harness it.

No, unless everyone is constantly reminded of the principles of alignment and it becomes part and parcel of their everyday life, then it won't ever truly happen for keeps.

The key to alignment is constant feedback. It is rather like how adults communicate with children. If you listen to any parent they are constantly saying; no don't do that. Or, if their offspring displays appropriate behaviour, they reinforce their approval with lavish helpings of praise and encouragement.

The adult brain is no different in many ways, except we have the benefit of more experience than a child and hopefully display more rational behaviour. We respond to the same stimuli. We repeat behaviour for which we get praise and shy away from doing things that earn us a reprimand. These are both useful techniques that a leader might want to bear in mind when he or she is maintaining the principles of alignment.

BUT, and this is a very big 'but' indeed, alignment is nothing whatsoever to do with performance reviews. In my opinion performance reviews should have been stopped when Noah found dry land. They are always a complete joke and, whatever advocates tell you, are rarely anything to do with reinforcing good behaviour and pointing out where a subordinate may have strayed off the path.

Over the years, in some organisations, performance management has developed into a discipline which is close to adversarial. Bosses treat it as an excuse to berate people for what they are not doing. They try to catch out their hapless victims for reasons that are beyond anyone's comprehension. Meanwhile, the person on the other end of the exercise generally sees it as an annual excuse to plead the case for a pay rise. Nothing more.

If you absolutely feel the need for a formal process, have a review. But, even then, there should be no surprises in the review because a team leader and their team will have been discussing performance *every* single week or at least every month. End of.

If a team is properly aligned, everyone should know what the plan is and they should know the part that they are playing in it. At the end of every month a team leader should be monitoring everyone's progress and together everyone should be addressing the parts of the plan which are not working, or where there is an obvious gap. There is no need for those destructive annual performance reviews because you should be in *constant* communication. You should never be in a situation where the boss suddenly brings up something that you did wrong a year before, or that 'the reason' your pay increase is a surprise. A disappointment maybe, but not a surprise.

Alignment is not something that is learned in a day or via an annual performance review 'pep talk'. You cannot harness a team's energy without constantly reinforcing the type of behaviour you require and challenging them to find new and better ways to hit their targets, every single day.

Get Aligned!

Alignment starts with getting everybody buying into the vision and where the key result areas (KRAs) will be in the short term.

The team leader should remind everyone:

- What the key strategic drivers of the business are
- What the main areas of focus are that will make the company successful

Then, he or she should ask the team:

- Where do we all need to be in order to make a significant difference?
- What are the KRAs we need to execute on and achieve to meet our goals?

Early on in the process, while everyone is still trying to get to grips with alignment, the team leader may get a range of answers. Most of them will probably concentrate on the area that the person answering the question is concerned with.

The KRAs you want, apply to the company as a whole.

So, make sure everyone understands;

- The measures of both their department *and* the team as a whole and how they are all linked together into the strategy
- How their own individual performance will impact the overall strategy

This all requires revisiting regularly. With the numerous diversions and challenges team members meet almost daily, revisiting monthly would be good but enough.

Hopefully, if you have been through 'plan and process' properly from chapter two, you will already have your three or four KRAs for the *whole* team.

These KRAs will have allowed you and your team to;

- Set your goals
- Make sure that each goal is both significant and measurable.

Now, you need to make sure that each member of the team is coming round to the notion of delivering in those KRAs *for the team* and not just focussing on *their own area of responsibility.*

Once the exacting performance goals are in place, the team needs to learn how to become comfortable with being vulnerable in front of their peers. This means that teams need to work at understanding the 'differences' between each other. We are not all the same and all manage our decisions in different ways. But, once we realize that we are on the same journey, cooperation will begin to happen and alignment is made easier.

It won't be easy, but if everyone is empowered to be honest with each other about their concerns, weaknesses and fears, it is the perfect starting point to begin engaging in a passionate dialogue around what is really important.

Having got this far in this book, I hope it will be no surprise for you to read that getting aligned begins at the top. A leader, of course, holds the key to building a high performing team. Not only do they lead the team to this point, but they then motivate and empower the team to make it happen. And keep happening.

Therefore, the team leader must:

- Link each of the measures above into a formal feedback and recognition system.
- Regularly review the goal performance and develop corrective actions to ensure that they are met.

Open awareness, trust and shared responsibility should be the watchwords for leaders when working at having their teams aligned.

At its simplest level, this may involve getting the team together and asking them who has seen something positive relating to the vision or values over the past four weeks. It is a perpetual reminder that everyone is working towards a mutual end point. Then, if no one has seen anything that relates to the vision or values, ask them why not? It is amazing how quickly the message starts to filter through. Alignment is not a one-day wonder.

Adopting a coaching culture will also continually clarify expectations between you and your individual team members.

Say to them; "Just because we said we are all going over there, I know that each of our interpretations of what that means is different. We are all starting at different grid references. So, tell me: what does that look like for you? Is there any way I can help you to adjust a bit?"

Accept that not everything will always be done the way you want it first time. Find a way to encourage the team in their endeavours, rather than criticise and belittle them.

Don't ever say; why did you do that like that? Or, worse still mutter about people behind their backs. Instead, ask people what is standing in the way of them delivering their goals. Take time out to consider whether people on the team are struggling with your communication. Get close to any that clearly are. Move into a coaching relationship and use coaching language with anyone who isn't aligned with what should be the modus operandi.

This is all possible, even if you are running a massive operation with offices all over the country, if not the world. Yes, there is an added layer of complexity in keeping a team aligned. You may hardly see your team face-to-face from one month to the next and it can be hard to find a structure that will keep the communication flowing. But, with some planning and organisation, the principles of alignment are just the same.

Start by setting the tone with a team-wide meeting at a central location. When you are all together, you can agree on the key results indicators and the vision for the future. That way, even if your team contact is subsequently only by phone for the main part, you will all have a common denominator. Everyone will know what needs to be done for the good of the company and will be motivated to do it. The team leader can do their job of reinforcing and motivating just the same. Webinars work, when you prepare for them.

A team leader of a high performing team needs to trust their own people and empower them to get on and take personal responsibility for the areas that they are responsible for whether they are in the same building, or 200 miles away. The most important thing is to continuously ensure that everyone is aligned with the overall goals. That may sometimes mean finding a new way to communicate with the team and maintain the momentum.

However, whatever the situation, it is never enough to just tell the team what the goals are and let them get on with it. A team leader needs to be constantly supportive and to create an open coaching culture. That is the basis for creating a high performing and fully aligned team.

I use an online web based tool with Teams (www.upagear.com u- online) which allows them to monthly score goals, monitor their progress with evolving their culture and communicate within the system to seek support when needed.

What to do when alignment is not happening

Take a moment to consider what might *really* be going on at an individual level when a team has considered its purpose, vision, mission and values. Outwardly everyone has bought into the notion of becoming a high performing team and is steadily working on building the important foundations for these goals.

Or are they?

As an exercise, why not ask the team to score their excitement and commitment level to the direction your purpose, vision, mission and values is now heading in after all your hard work. Use a scale of one to ten, with ten meaning it is going really, really well and everyone is champing at the bit to make this work. A score of one means it is a real dog's dinner. Chances are, unless something has gone very wrong, you will probably get a very positive range of scores between eight out of ten to a more-than-respectable full marks.

Then ask everyone on the team to fill in the following statement with the first thing that comes into their minds. Encourage them to be totally honest:

> *"I am motivated by these very positive purpose, vision, mission and values, but......"*

This exercise, when done properly, will never fail to expose at least half a dozen limiting mindsets. It will also show the team leader why, even though they have a clear vision, the team is not heading towards it with the pace that might be expected or hoped for.
Yes, your team may have been hyped up by the workshop you held to discuss your goals, saying to all and sundry what a positive day it had been. But, after they have returned to their silos to get on with their 'own' work, it will not take long for the cracks to appear, for the behaviours which support the limiting beliefs to play out.

Doing this will also provide very clear proof that the various members of the team actually have very different levels of attachment to the vision and are, in fact, far from fully aligned. Indeed, the team is not aligned at all.

What has gone wrong?

To get to the bottom of this, it may help to go back a stage and consider the widely recognized definition of a team:

A small number of people with complementary skills who are committed to a common purpose, performance goals and working approach for which they hold themselves mutually accountable.[2]

---

[2] The Wisdom of Teams, Katzenback and Smith, Harper Business 1994.

Remember, this is not a definition of a *high performing* team. It is simply a team. Then think about this statement in terms of your team and indeed any team you have ever worked with in your past. I am sure you will agree that the part about holding themselves 'mutually accountable' is actually a rarity.

The truth is, for most people, common purpose is all very well, just as long as it does not encroach on *their* own area of responsibility too much. They are not being deliberately obstructive, or lazy. Nor are they incompetent.

In fairness, it is a tough ask to get any team to fully commit their time and energy to purpose, vision, mission and values. In a very basic way, they took on their job to do sales, or marketing, or accounts, or whatever role they were recruited for. Now, suddenly, they apparently have this extra role (or unpaid job as they may view it) as a 'team player'. That new addition to their job description may seem pretty daunting, particularly if they think they've got quite a lot on their plate as it is. In a demanding role, people, quite understandably, get distracted by business as usual.

All of this is before you even consider that each individual on a senior team probably has a pretty strong ego, or they wouldn't have got that far up the career ladder. Now somebody is asking them to suppress that natural instinct to look after number one, in order to improve *everyone's* performance.

The task of a team leader is to prove to the team that, when they become aligned, they will get more time to do their 'day' job, not less. It is no easy task, which is why it is not performed over-night and requires continual monitoring and reinforcement.

How alignment helps us to reach our goals

My favourite example of alignment was working with a team of seven including the leader. The business had battled for survival during the credit crunch period and a couple of new, stronger people had recently joined the team. Each member of the team were determined people and four of them were very strong characters indeed. When I met them they had been together for four months and change was very much in the air, along with strong 'views' as to what needed to happen in each of their silos and where others needed to adjust.

When we first met as a team for a two day offsite session, one of the discussions we had was around alignment. They concurred that they probably only scored a six out of 10 on alignment, but admitted the results were variable. Three months later, with an inspiring vision in place, and the values they created being communicated everywhere and progress on their annual goals looking good, they not only scored their alignment as nine out of 10, they declared :

- We are getting more done
- It is enjoyable working as a team in our meetings
- We feel genuinely supported in everything we are responsible for
- I feel safe and supported 'opening up' to concerns

Now, that is something to be proud of!

PRACTICAL GUIDE to CREATING and SUSTAINING ALIGNMENT:

- Alignment is never done. It is never finished
- The key is finding a proper structural framework and promoting a genuine culture of understanding and trust
- That means fostering communication skills which concentrate on the production of extraordinary relationships
- Alignment is the harmonious way to delivering the results you want
- Powerful working relationships are *everyone's* responsibility- it is these which will create time (saved from unconstructive meeting discussion) to allow innovation to be more readily acceptable.
- Make sure 'Team Player' is in every Job Description and that you explain why from time to time.
- Recognise that 'aligning' may not be comfortable for everyone – we do not have to agree on all Team decisions or direction but we do have to align!

Chapter five - Values

Ask any group of people what makes a good team and the chances are that most will come back and declare that it has a 'common set of values' and they live by them. By which they mean; an implicit agreement about the code by which they live and work together. Interestingly, exceptionally successful sporting Coaches Alex Ferguson of Manchester United and Bill Walsh of the San Fransisco 49ers indirectly support that. They have each authored books on 'Leadership' where they place enormous emphasis on 'Standards' – an overarching value which is pursuing excellence.

Which all sounds great in theory. The problem is, like so many of these gung ho, catch-all, statements, no one really understands what they mean. Still less do they get what it has to do with them.

Worse still, it usually just isn't true.

In truth, people's values are very personal to them and often bear little resemblance to those of their colleagues.

Some values are inherited – if your mum and dad worked hard to get what they wanted, chances are you will be prepared to put your nose to the grindstone if you want to get anywhere.

Some values are learned – often the hard way.

Some values reflect the aspirations of your generation – because we always know better than our predecessors. Or so we think.

Some values are simply a reflection of the place where we have lived most of our lives – because city folk often count themselves as more worldly wise than country folk and vice versa.

My own values were predominantly formed from my time in army training at Sandhurst. While there, I learned about the importance of time keeping, mainly because if I did not deliver what I had to do within the required timescale I was sorely scolded. Plus, I let the rest of my team down, which in the army is unforgiveable. Personal responsibility and accountability were also drummed into me there – values that live with me today.

These values became so embedded that, when I left the army to embark on a career in sales, I worked in a completely different way from my colleagues who had vastly different backgrounds.

On my initial training course for the commission only job I was told that if I made twenty calls a day, five days a week, I would end up with twelve to fifteen appointments. Eight of those appointments would keep the meeting and the rest would either not show up, or change their minds and send me away. Out of those remaining eight, I might expect to make two sales, which would hopefully produce the commission I needed to live on.

So that is what I did. Relentlessly, day after day. What really drove me on was that I always felt that someone was watching me to see if I was sticking to my work- my Army values! Indeed, I even imagined that someone was following me around the streets of Bristol, checking that I was on target! They weren't of course. It is just that my own values of 'hard work pays' were so firmly entrenched that they shaped my every move. But, as a result, I got those sales and quickly became one of the top sellers in the branch, easily outstripping my colleagues who were a bit more laid back in their approach. I have remained the same in every single job I have ever tackled since.

The point of relating this tale is to show that our values can last a lifetime and manifest themselves in everything we do. Yes, these values may change a little as we mature but, fundamentally, they are pretty stable. Equally I have seen Teams adopt Values to suit the business and over time watched individuals, individually and collectively create the habits of living them to their joint enjoyment.

So, the question to ask yourself is this: do you still think that everyone on your team, from diverse backgrounds and cultures, is really living the same values?

Yes, a high performing team is all about harnessing the powers of synergy and teamwork, but it would be a huge mistake to assume that, because a group of people are aligned behind the vision and purpose, they have somehow automatically adopted complementary values too. They haven't. Unless you take the time to articulate the values of the individual members and then define a clear set of values for the team, you won't ever come close to being able to take full advantage of their combined intelligence, energy, enthusiasm and personal commitment.

It would not be over egging it to say: finding the values for your team represents the *biggest* single opportunity a leader has to evolve true teamwork.

Too many companies make the mistake of assuming that everyone knows and understands the core values of the organisation, without ever bothering to check. They think that everyone has, as a matter of course, bought into these values and lives them every day. Indeed, the very fact that some businesses have printed their values out, framed them and then displayed them prominently behind the reception desk is testament to the fact that they are rather taking things for granted.

What happens? Everyone gets confused, ignores the framed missive and follows their own path. After all, when there is nothing bigger or better to serve (or at least nothing obvious), people will always self-serve.

The differentiators are the teams who actually *live* the values. Decisions are made easier and faster and trust grows more quickly too. A focus on the important is natural in teams who abide by and truly do live their values.

Values are the glue that holds all the other elements together through good and tough times. Values, like vision, always ensure that it is abundantly clear that there is something greater to serve.

Effective, high performing, teams have a clear, shared purpose and a vision for the future. They also share a specific set of core values and are energetic in behaving them.

We need to understand each other's values because

Imagine two colleagues who are both carrying out broadly the same tasks. One person takes a whole week to finish the job, but the result is as near perfect as you could ever hope for. The other completes it in half the time, but although the end product works OK, it just isn't the absolute, finest, 100 per cent right, piece of work you might like from your team.

The first person, whose values are based on doing a thorough, perfect and expert job, will become constantly frustrated by what they see as their colleague's slipshod attitude. Meanwhile, his colleague, who values efficiency and fast work, will inevitably believe that his co-worker is just too slow and plodding to be a useful team member.

If no previous direction has been laid out as to the way the company values the speed or quality of work, neither of these colleagues is 'right' or 'wrong', nor indeed is one better than the other. They are just different. They have different values. Most teams are like this and people on such teams usually automatically gravitate towards those with similar values. Thus, our fast-working friend above will praise colleagues to the hilt who complete things quickly just like him and will be utterly disparaging about others who do not. He, or she, will therefore be fully aligned with some of his colleagues, but will never see eye-to-eye with the slower moving perfectionists. Meanwhile those perfectionists on the team will be gathering for regular despairing chats about their slapdash co-workers.

But, as we have already seen, in order for a team to become a high performing team, 100 per cent alignment is needed. Anything else simply means performance is being eroded and valuable energy is being wasted.

If people can be helped to understand that different people will work to differing values, they can learn to support and help one another. Once you have that support and understanding, alignment will follow. Then, instead of wasting time bad-mouthing each other to colleagues and eroding team unity, people will be able to work together, complimenting each other's strengths and weaknesses.

Once a team understands each other's values, and that they can and will be different, they will then be able to find complimentary values that can be established as values that the team as a whole can follow. Developing those team values will shape the way the organisation works in the future and provides a guiding light as to which behaviours are crucial to the team's success.

When you articulate the values respected by the team it will act like a stake in the ground, declaring to everyone what is and isn't acceptable, why it is important in underpinning Vision, Strategy customer satisfaction, how we treat our people – everything we are here for.

Values are not about...

Profit

Profit is not a value. It is a goal! All businesses (even non-profit making ones) have to make money just to survive, just as a human being needs oxygen to live. But, oxygen and money are not the reason for existing.

They are not values.

The most successful teams don't focus on sales and profits. They stand for something bigger. That said, it is worth bearing in mind that a company where the team is focussed on something and working together is usually highly profitable.

Shared values are....

The only thing that works is management by values. Find people who are competent and really bright, but more importantly who care exactly about the same things as you care about.

Steve Jobs
Co Founder, Apple

Shared team values are about the culture we want to encourage, the standards we should have and the principles that should underpin the efforts of the team. Whilst most other things can change over time, values should hold true whatever the weather or circumstance. They are a team's unifying core and will inform your leadership style without compromise.

Shared values:

- Engender trust and link the team together
- Create the identity by which this team is known by all its stakeholders

Indeed, a value driven team will tap into your greatest sources of energy and inspiration.

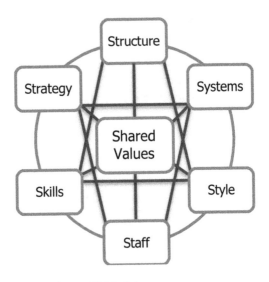

Figure 5: The McKinsey 7S Model

One of the most enduring models of organisational effectiveness is the McKinsey 7S Framework, which was developed in the early 1980s by consultants Tom Peters and Robert Waterman. The basic idea of the model is that there are seven internal aspects of a business that need to be aligned if the organisation is to be successful.

Take a look at the centre of the model. Shared values are at the heart of everything. They touch on absolutely everything because they are positively central to the development of all the other critical elements. Any company's structure, systems, style, staff, skills and strategy *all* stem from why the organisation was originally created and what it stands for.

When any company is first started, the vision for that business stems from the values of its creators. Then, as those values change or develop along the way, so do all the other elements from strategy to style.

In an ideal world, everyone recruited to a team would arrive with the same set of values. But, as we have already seen, that is pretty unlikely. The next best thing therefore, is to understand each individual's values, share them to understand where everyone is coming from and then get the whole team on the same page with the team's values which will support the realisation of the vision.

To do this, you must find answers to the following questions:

- What are the team's core values?
- What is the corporate/team culture?
- How strong are the values?

Once you ascertain these shared values, it is quite likely that they will not be natural to everyone. They are, in all likelihood, not the values that people have grown up with, but with a little persistence and hard work, people will begin to accept them. Once the team is no longer frightened of the shared values, that is when the magic of alignment begins. Decisions will be made faster and it will be easier to get things back on track when they go awry. Colleagues will be more willing to prompt each other when they spot something that goes against the shared values and, equally, will be quick to praise each other when a value is upheld.

Being congratulated and appreciated makes people feel good. When we get praised, we endeavour to do more of what has elicited this positive response. Values drive behaviour, which in turn drives results. Get the values right and action and profit will follow.

A team where everyone believes the same thing and shares the same values will get the results they want.

Finding personal values among individual team members

Unlike all the exercises so far in this book, finding the team values does not come from the top. While a team leader should instigate the definition and articulation of values, this process hinges on individual team members revealing their own values. Until this is done, it is very difficult to move the process on to get a greater team understanding and cooperation and define team values for everyone to align behind.

Schedule a meeting and ask the team to read through the twenty values listed below and rank them from one (most important) to twenty (least important).

Score

	Score	
1	( )	Achievement (sense of accomplishment)
2	( )	Adventure (exploration, risks, excitement)
3	( )	Personal freedom (independence, choices)
4	( )	Authenticity (being frank and genuine)
5	( )	Expertness (having full grasp of something)
6	( )	Emotional health (able to handle inner feelings)
7	( )	Service (contributing to others)
8	( )	Leadership (having influence and authority)
9	( )	Money (financial security, savings)
10	( )	Spirituality (meaning to life, religious belief)
11	( )	Physical health (vitality)
12	( )	Meaningful work (relevant and purposeful job)
13	( )	Affection (caring, giving and receiving love)
14	( )	Pleasure (enjoyment, satisfaction, fun)
15	( )	Wisdom (mature understanding, insight)
16	( )	Family (happy and contented living situation)
17	( )	Recognition (being well-known, praised)
18	( )	Security (have a secure and stable future)
19	( )	Self-growth (self-exploration and development)
20	( )	Mental health (having a keen, active mind)

The 'force rating' aspect to this exercise is very important because the team may well be reticent to reveal their true values. Most people find it hard to select values based on behaviours i.e. what they do and instead try to second-guess the exercise by rating what they think they should value. However, if they have to give each one a ranking between one and twenty, it means they will have to think hard about their own values because they can't have them all as number one. Each one must have its own ranking. By doing it this way, it forces people to get to grips with the true picture and should give a fairly accurate list of the top five values for each member of the team.

It might help to concentrate the mind, if the people tackling the list are asked to consider each value on the basis of how it is demonstrated in their everyday lives. This self-referencing process is a useful skill and will also help prepare the participant for the next stage.

Having done this valuable work, get the whole team together to discuss each other's values. Pick out at least one value from everyone's list and look at it in more depth. Let people articulate how the value applies in their day-to-day lives and brainstorm how else these values might manifest themselves.

Inevitably, the lists of each individual member will be different. The great thing is, now everyone is aware that their colleagues have different values and agendas, and have acknowledged and discussed them, it opens the way to more openness in the team. By defining these personal values, it makes it easier for everyone to make a personal connection with the next part in this process, that of attaching people to team values.

Translating personal values into shared values

The three key steps to developing shared values are:
- Determine what is really important
- Explain the behaviours and actions required to put each value into action
- Account for any gaps between where we are now and where we want to be

The process should kick off with a discussion of the team's vision, mission and strategic intent and current key result areas. It may help to put a statement of the team vision on display in the room, together with the lists of values documented in the individual top fives. Then, start by discussing common values that the team could live by in order to realise the vision of the future that they have previously agreed upon.

The values could be any from the following list, and more:

Dependability	Flexibility	Compassion
Ambition	Respect	Innovation
Competency	Dedication	Teamwork
Individuality	Diversity	Excellence
Equality	Improvement	Accountability
Integrity	Fun	Empowerment
Service	Loyalty	Quality
Responsibility	Credibility	Efficiency
Accuracy	Honesty	Collaboration
Courage	Influence	Challenge
Leadership	Tidy	Entrepreneurial

Taking each value one at a time, begin by defining what some of these values mean to people individually. Then, go on to define how each one might apply to the group as a whole. Or not. List any strong contenders on a flip chart or board. Encourage people to consider how each particular value is currently demonstrated in the organisation. Better still, open a dialogue as to what happens when that value *isn't* demonstrated.

Repeat this process until a list of critical shared values for the whole team begins to emerge. Then, take as much time as needed to whittle the list down to the five key values which most closely tie in with the vision. It may take more than one session to do this. That's fine. The important thing is getting it right.

Leading the discussion to align on the most important values is a critical role and does require facilitating with care. Take care not to suggest ideas or take sides. It is not unknown for organizations to select values which they 'thought they ought to have', rather than actually being in full support of their direction.

If you end up with a list of values that 'look good' or are simply a way of second-guessing what the team leaders might want, you'll end up worse off than if you had never bothered. The next stage in this mindset is; well, those values didn't work. To which, the answer is: of course they didn't! The values were not a real reflection of the team, nor were they grounded in where they wanted to go. These values were sunk before they even left the room.

I once worked with a team responsible for the UK arm of a global organization who decided they needed new values to support their inspiring and challenging vision of the future. Five of the eight person team stuck rigidly to the argument that they had to have 'Integrity' as one of their five values. It took some time to get through to them that, by excluding 'integrity, it didn't mean it was OK for the organization to lack integrity. It was simply that it was not in the top five values necessary for this team to excel – their values were for behaving not for show and integrity was to be a given. Indeed, as it turned out, the values they actually chose to realise their demanding vision were; credibility, execution, innovation, energy and teamwork. These values were perfect for this team and provided just the support to the vision they hankered for. I don't think they would have ever achieved that if they had stuck to 'integrity'.

As any team edits and refines their list, there may well be extensive discussion and argument among the group. That's great. In fact, the more challenge the better. The more people examine the relative merits of particular values, the more likely they are to remember the ones they have agreed upon and why.

Remind the team: When they become genuinely value-driven it will realise the full potential, possibility and energy of all the individuals in the group, regardless of their personal values. By articulating and then aligning behind team values, people will begin to work together more effectively. They will be connected.

Defining values together and agreeing to a group-wide definition will make a powerful connection among the team. It will also make them focus on what is really important to the whole shape and culture of the team.

You will have picked up by now that it is ' behaving' the Team or Corporate Values that individually and the organisation profit in a variety of ways. Processes and Meetings are efficient and positive, customers and staff see and feel benefits.

When I am Performance Coaching Teams I ALWAYS have them create a simple template as follows.

(Diagram to fit here...................)

The team members input real examples of both the Behaviors and the Outcomes. It is not unusual for us to discuss that document every month. It is critical that the document is shared at EVERY level of the organisation. I know several organisations who provide specific rewards to individuals who are 'caught' going the 'extra mile' so to speak in behaving the Values.

Getting ready to apply those values

Defining the shared values is, however, only the start of the journey. Values should not be reduced to being yet another inspiring list to be pasted up behind the reception desk, along with the vision and mission statement. They have to become part of the day-to-day language of the team.

Take, for example, a time when the team reaches a deadlock, or simply can't make a decision over the best way forward. Ask them to consider the issue in the context of the values that were agreed in the earlier exercise. Does the problem look different now? You bet it does.

Align a decision with the values and you will be amazed how the mists suddenly clear. Filter choices through the values test and the truth will always emerge.

It will get easier over time too. When the whole team honours the agreed values, it proves a powerful binding force during times of potential stress and conflict. They are a constant reminder of the common ground shared by the team. It is only when a team focuses on the truly important, that they will excel.

Lose sight of the values and you will lose out.

I once worked with a construction company which did just that and lost a multi-million pound contract with a major supermarket group as a result. In the soul searching which followed the failed tender, the answers to all their questions came down to just one thing; the company had lost sight of its values and suffered because of it. While its values statement declared that service, achievement, exceeding expectations and attention to detail were ingrained in the company culture, they weren't. Over the years the statement had become like wallpaper with no one paying it attention and, indeed, many newcomers to the company were not even aware of it. So, when the invitation to tender came in, no one saw that it was a priority to pull their best people away from what they were doing to concentrate on the vital tender. No one spoke up and offered vital resources to the bid. No one saw that this was a looming problem. As a result, the tender fell a long way short of what they could have produced if they had but heeded their values and, hardly surprisingly, the business went to a company that was more fleet of foot.

This is why it is absolutely bedrock vital to constantly remind everyone of the shared values. I don't mean with the ubiquitous sign in reception. Or just in times of strife. I mean with constant communication.

So:

- Attach it to the agenda for meetings
- Ask people how what they have just done demonstrates the company values…
- ….Or, why it doesn't
- Put those values in front of everyone in the team. Every day.
- Ask them; how are you doing? …
- … What is the proof that this action or that one demonstrates our shared values?

Do this and living the shared values will become second nature, just as they should be.

Ditch the limiting mind-sets

Once you have agreed that all-important list of five team values, some members of the team might well say; but those are not my personal values. In fact they are nothing like *my* values. The answer to this reaction is that; these are the values that the team as a whole has agreed that they must adopt in order to meet the inspiring vision of the future. These values, whether or not they are everyone's core, personal, values are what are required in order for individuals and the team as a whole to realise the vision. It is up to everyone to recognise these team values and to find a way of adopting them and aligning behind them. It might be a challenge, but who ever said creating, and being a member of, a high performing team would be easy?

Ideally, of course, an individual's values will be closely aligned to the team's shared values. People naturally gravitate to companies which display similar cultural beliefs to their own and when this is borne out, it makes people happier and more energised.

If this is not the case though, team members with miss-matched values must be afforded every opportunity to understand and embrace the shared values. If they cannot buy into the shared values it will erode performance and sap the energy of other team members. A leader's job will be made easier in helping this endeavour along, if they have laid the groundwork for alignment, as discussed earlier in this book. If, for example, one of the core shared values is openness and honesty and yet one member of the team believes that the best way to get on is to play a resolutely political game, it will stand out a mile. Yes, the natural style of a political-style player is to keep their hand close to their chest and try to get things changed in a subversive way, but if the basics of alignment are in place, it is quite possible they can be helped to see how their behaviour is impeding the process of the team as a whole. Some well-chosen coaching words could easily get them on side if they are already predisposed to trust their colleagues. Failing that, they may well need to be moved on to another team which better suits their personal values.

How values help us meet our goals

Early on during my Team working with a firm of nuclear engineers, I started talking to the chief executive about values. He turned to me and said in all earnestness: "This sort of thing doesn't work. We are, by nature, a cynical bunch we engineers."

The problem that this firm had was, as with so many companies, the bosses had diligently written out the company values (as they saw them) and put them on the website and in a frame in the boardroom. That was as far as it went. After a while, even those that were aware of them, forgot that they existed.

Once I worked with the team and together they formed a realistic set of meaningful values, the transformation was breath-taking.

As the chief executive later told me: *"The movers and shakers ended up walking the talk and guarding their values in all that they did. In tough competitive circumstances we were unstoppable."*

It is no coincidence that within a very short space of time this highly focussed team trebled the value of the business. I enjoyed very much the request from the chief executive several years later, to talk to a new team about the financial benefits of shared team values. However, I resisted the temptation to say: I told you so!

Once they found their values and learned the value in behaving them, they clearly hadn't done that badly for a cynical bunch of engineers.

PRACTICAL GUIDE to MAKING VALUES WORK for you and YOUR TEAM:

- They are not a dry list left mouldering in the corner – a team has to live the values constantly
- They are a guide to what is really important which can be referred to again and again if there are any gaps between where we are now and where we should be
- They hold the key to unlocking complex problems, or guiding the way in tricky decisions
- Values should be discussed regularly at executive meetings.
- Where individuals do not naturally fit with a particular Value – work with them (Coach) over a period of time to have them (and the Team) benefit from inculcating a new habit into their repertoire of talent.
- Remember , finding the Values for your Team and working them daily in tandem with your Vision represents the biggest single opportunity a leader has to evolve true Teamwork…
- Be brave and proud in communicating your Values to all stakeholders.

Chapter six - Rigid flexibility

Things were going pretty well in my work with the UK arm of a global engineering business. It was a relatively small subsidiary, with a turnover of $10 million, but the general manager was keen that he and his team made a mark, so he had called me in to advise him on getting everyone up to speed. After I had met him and then begun to dig a little deeper through my initial meetings with the team, it turned out that although there were some good people there, some fast revitalization was required.

So, we all began the journey together. Beginning with a two day off-site meeting, where we created an inspiring vision of the future, settled on the team values and agreed a great plan, we started the process of working through it all, month-by-month.

Two months into the process, with everything apparently on track, one of the team members approached me at the end of one of our regular half-day team meetings.

"Can you let us know the programme for the remainder of the year?" he asked.

I hesitated for a moment, because I knew that the answer that I was going to give him was not going to be the one he might have wanted. But, I have always believed honesty is the best policy, so I gave it to him straight.

"There isn't one," I replied.

Then, seeing that this probably wouldn't be enough, I added; "Our aim, together, is to lift this team's performance considerably and for you all to be enjoying your roles at work."

As I has expected, my inquisitor clearly was not satisfied.

"Oh come on," he exclaimed, feigning complete exasperation.

"Surely you must have *some* idea!"

It was at this point that I had to explain the theory of rigid flexibility which is something all teams must fully understand and embrace if they are ever to stand a chance of becoming a high performing team.

At the centre of my argument for adopting rigid flexibility is the fact that nobody can truly ever have any idea of what is coming at them over the next hill. You may remember that earlier in the Plan and Process chapter I mentioned the old army expression; no plan survives first contact with the enemy? Well, it is true and that is why this saying has been so full-heartedly adopted and embraced by sports teams and forward-thinking businesses the world over. It doesn't matter how hard you train, or imagine that your opponent/customer will do this, that or the other, if you are not prepared something will always happen that will completely surprise you.

It doesn't matter what the plan is, whether you are lining-up for the final of the Rugby World Cup, or running an electronics firm in Edgebaston and agreeing goals for the year ahead. If you make a plan, however detailed and impressive, things will change. Once that first ball is kicked, or everyone returns to their desks, things will never proceed down an orderly route. If you don't embrace that fact, it will be hugely frustrating to you and everyone around you.

In one of my early executive roles in a FTSE250 firm back in the Seventies, the company used to spend days honing its plans as it looked forward to where to take the organization over the next three years and, in particular, what needed to be done over the next 12 months. This meticulous operation would involve a three day planning offsite every year which all the executives would attend. At the end of this process, everyone's thoughts would be gathered together and proudly turned into a fat and impressive looking document.

Very often though, that document would not see the light of day for any meaningful reference, from one year's planning meeting to the next.

Why was this happening, I asked myself? It was admirable that this firm was committed to introducing fresh thinking every year and airing forthcoming challenges through this process. I liked the fact that they were dedicated to producing concrete annual goals. But, why did no one on the team from the man at the top to the team below ever see it through?

Where it all fell apart was; once we all got back to our desks we could plainly see how rapidly this rigid plan went off track and lost its relevance. The moment it came into contact with the realities of the daily grind, the hourly changes in the market place and the demands of the stock market, it just did not seem sustainable. With the plan becoming less and less applicable by the minute, everyone involved naturally abandoned it and got on with doing their best to battle with the new challenges.

The problem was that my company's plan did not allow for any rigid flexibility. If only I had known then what I know now, which is that: High performing teams have to be at ease with the principle of rigid flexibility.

Rigid flexibility is a careful balance of two key principles:

1. **Rigid** – a team must achieve what it has committed to make happen for all of its stakeholders.
2. **Flexibility** – at the same time, a team has to be open to challenge and being challenged. This means a plan could be changed to use fewer resources, or, at the other end of the scale, there will be a requirement to substantially add to the workload to get it done. Occasionally, there may even be a need to stop a previously well argued-for project altogether while the circumstances are re-assessed.

We need rigid flexibility because:

Plans don't always work!

According to research[3], the average team achieves only 63 per cent of the objectives of their strategic plans. Or, looking at it the other way, that is a whopping 37 per cent that don't go to plan. What gets in the way?

Plans fail because:

- The projections agreed at the outset were unrealistic, or lacked key elements of research, or

---

[3] Michael C Mankins and Richard Steele, Turning strategy into great performance, Harvard Business Review, August 2005

simply did not (or could not) fill in the 'unknowns' at that time.

- Poor communication and follow through gradually erode the original aim, rather like a lengthy game of corporate Chinese whispers.
- Top management fail to notice performance bottlenecks – and no team members in the ranks below point them out.
- No one 'owns' the plan and therefore it is not properly tracked against the annual goals.
- Culturally, teams are not yet at ease with ambiguity and constant change.

There is also the problem of limiting paradigms among the individuals on the team, which, collectively, can kill off a plan. These limiting paradigms on a person-by-person basis can be:

- Other priorities get in the way, such as pressing demands of the 'day job'
- Everyone thinks it is someone else's job to fulfil the plan
- They understand the plan, but find their part in it too difficult
- They don't understand the plan – but are too afraid to ask for clarification

As we have seen many times in this book, all teams possess limiting mindsets which act as roadblocks to progress. Typically, in plans, it is the most damaging limiting paradigm which causes a lack of flexibility, indeed reinforces the rigidity of negative or no longer pertinent behaviour. They therefore restrict the team and its ability to perform in a way that will deliver the desired results.

I once worked as a consultant for a company in the banking sector, which like all other firms in the financial services field, was massively impacted by the credit crunch. This particular organization was never reduced to the status of state ownership, however, the team I was working with did find itself having to significantly sharpen its weekly and monthly financial proposals to the board in response to the extraordinary events of the downturn. These proposals were for very complex deals based upon eye-watering amounts of money upon which decisions from the board were required swiftly. There was also the added pressure that decisions were having to be made in an incredibly fluid market which was literally changing minute-by-minute.

The team in question kept on hitting a wall of requests from the board for more and more information, all of which required an incredible amount of detail to answer. As a result, most of the people on this 24-person team were working crippling 20-hour days and, even so, frequently missing out on some of the deals.

By taking the leadership team out of the maelstrom for a few hours one day, we were able to identify a number of limiting paradigms that existed among them. The most damaging paradigm of them all was:

"We have to answer all of the board's questions in exhausting detail in order to gain their confidence and trust."

This, we identified, was at the core of why they were working in such a rigid and unrewarding way. It was also why they were working themselves into the ground working twice their normal hours. A lack of flexibility in any aspect of their job was slowing down the team to a virtual standstill and actually putting the entire organization at risk because they were losing out on deals.

The solution for the team was to turn their limiting belief on its head to:

"We are trusted to make the best and safest deal recommendations."

Did it work? Well, yes it did. The change was not instantaneous, but it helped the team to adopt a fresh, more flexible, approach to the way they worked. They concentrated on the parts of the proposals that really counted and added value and reduced the amount of time on the bits that didn't really add very much at all. Some individuals became really energized by the possibilities that the new mindset might bring – soon, the hours being worked were more rewarding and enjoyable and later, the hours at work reduced dramatically. Over time, this resulted in the board becoming more confident in giving their approvals faster because they could cut to the chase and immediately see the salient parts. This, in turn, reduced the frustrations in the team and helped them to be even quicker on their feet. Plus, seeing as they were not longer working through the night, they were refreshed enough to do their job to the best of their abilities.

Therefore, in this context, the team fulfilled both sides of rigid flexibility:

Rigidity – The team had to do the deals.
Flexibility – They had to learn to communicate differently to the past.

Learning to balance the two elements was the key to unlocking the strength and productivity of this high performing team.

Rigid flexibility is....

The art of being flexible and adaptive by empowering all levels of the team to make decisions, even at the lowest level.

Returning to the well-known adage of no plan surviving first contact with the enemy, there is much that can be learned from the military when it comes to rigid flexibility.

Over the years and through various bloody campaigns, necessity has impelled the forces to hone this acceptance that events will change and generally do. It is hardwired into anyone in the services that there needs to be a process in place to react to these changes.

The solution, which centres on the concept of 'mission command', holds some valuable lessons for those in the corporate world.

At the heart of mission command is the necessity of establishing a high degree of alignment behind the *what* and the *why*, and then to devolve a substantial amount of decision-making authority further down the ranks as to the question of the *how*. Therefore, rather than simply following detailed orders, it is an officer's responsibility to understand the intention of his superiors and then take whatever action he deems necessary to fulfil it. In a combat situation, young leaders are trained to go forward according to the plan, yet react with appropriate flexibility the moment they encounter an hitherto unknown situation. They appreciate the situation fast, consider the alternatives and respond with speed, clarity, confidence and safety. If things change – as they no doubt will – that officer's guide to his or her future action is the *original* intent of the plan.

In the corporate world, this idea of giving the power of decision-making to those who need it, is known as empowerment. Apart from motivating all concerned, it speeds up everything because information does not have to be passed up and down the line before anything can be done. It means the individual who has the most up to date information can react quickly, adjust his or her plan and adapt to circumstances.

One of the most important lessons to be learned here is the team leader does not have to take responsibility for walking everyone past the various obstacles that come up. His or her job is to convey where the team needs to get to and then to give the team the means to get there.

In my experience, this is the thing many leaders find most difficult to do.

I recently spent many weeks coaching a deputy managing director of a large insurance firm. Early on in the process, I asked him what he felt that a successful outcome from this process would be.

He told me that he wanted to have an inspirational impact on his team and the clients, while also building a profitable business model.

What was he doing about it? I asked.

Well, he said, he was talking to two or three of his key people to get their views on the current road blocks to progress and, having heard what they said, was then planning to go away and come up with a solution.

To me though, this was completely missing the point. What he should have been doing is gathering everyone around him, getting them to air what the problems were with fulfilling the plan and then getting *them* to come up with the solution.

Leadership is, after all, achieving your goals by harnessing the efforts of other people.

If this team leader could look at it in this way, he would be able to see that rigid flexibility is as much about not feeling responsible for coming up with the ideas, as recognising that it is about achieving the end game. It doesn't matter who comes up with the bright ideas, or who moves the road block, as long as the team achieves the original objective.

Figure 6: Changing direction is sometimes the right thing to do

Finding your team's rigid flexibility

When plans are made, people always make forecasts and assumptions based on current conditions. But, as we all know, those conditions can (and do) change by the hour.

There is not much use hoping they don't because hoping is not an effective strategy.

It is impossible to plan for every contingency. Indeed, trying too hard to do this can paralyze everything as a team grinds to a halt trying to second-guess everything. However, there are ways a high performing team can be as ready as possible for the unexpected and also open to adapting should things change.

The key is to make sure every plan undergoes a 'what if' process to discuss possible things that might go wrong and their potential impact on the original plan.

Areas the team may like to consider are:

Internal
- **Personnel.** What would happen to your plans if a key member of the senior team leaves? No amount of key man insurance can make up for the loss of this experience and knowledge. If this person was instrumental to the plan, it could leave a huge gap and without contingency planning it would take months to get someone else up to speed.
- **Infrastructure.** Will your internal structures, such as IT or manufacturing capabilities, support this plan, both in the early stages and when it is ramped up to full capacity?

External
- **Economy.** After the recent global financial meltdown, we all now know we can't take anything for granted. However, teams still do. If you produce one, five, or even ten, year projections as though they were cast in stone, you are going to be in for a big disappointment.

- **Customers.** Don't assume that because your customers all love you now, it will ever be thus whatever you do. It won't. All businesses are cyclical and consumers are notoriously fickle.

- **Competitors.** Do you really think that your arch rival is going to just sit there and take it while you try to steal a march on them? Meanwhile, very often while you and your long-term competitor are duelling for business, a younger, fitter, more fleet of foot business will slip by while no one is looking. It happens all the time.

- **Regulation/legislation.** Who knows what might be coming around the corner? Rules change all the time. If your success is based on pending actions from the current administration, you could be in real trouble if the environment changes.

What iffing is a great attitudinal approach and a habit all high performing teams need to adopt. In fact, if a team regularly what ifs, it is a sure sign it *is* a high performing team. The team members are comfortable with being positively challenging. Thanks to the other characteristics of a high performing team covered in this book, such as trust and alignment, no one considers it a negative to raise potential barriers to progress.

If John says; 'What if Bill's IT department has not got the capacity to deal with this goal?', Bill doesn't see it as a personal sleight. He'll agree that this could be an issue and together the team will work out a way to beef up the IT side so it can cope. It won't cross Bill's mind that John is trying to undermine him – and that is because John isn't. They are all in it together and what iffing is simply the best way forward.

A team may not get everything covered in their what iffing, indeed, it is highly likely that they won't. However, by adopting this mindset they will be flexible enough and able to think fast on their feet to deal with pretty much anything that might happen.

Maintaining the momentum

Many businesses get wedded to the fact that, if you make a plan, you should stick to it come hell or high water. It is part of believing in what they do. But, think about your own business. Compare your plan of, say, five years ago to one you would write now. Even a year ago it would probably be markedly different. As you have lived the business from day-to-day, things have changed and it is the canny business person that changes with it. Constantly.

I have a client in the building trade whose firm really suffered in the credit crunch, as did most of the sector. The main thrust of their plan, before the financial meltdown, was to target a handful of really large contracts, rather than bringing in dozens of small ones. So, the team duly went off to pitch for all the big construction jobs in the UK. They went hell for leather for one massive job in the south east and were up against some stiff competition. They eventually won the contract by paring their margins back to the bone, so they would be earning practically zero on the job, but comforted themselves with the hope that they might be able to claw back some of it along the way.

Then the credit crisis hit.

It soon became apparent that not only would they not be able to claw back any money from their biggest contract, they were actually losing cash every day their builders went on site. Every time they bought the new materials they needed it sent them further into debt. My client faced a stark choice; rethink the plan fast, or sink into administration.

Being a highly driven and forward thinking bunch, they chose the former option and immediately reverted to targeting those small jobs which they had turned their backs on earlier. If it meant that they were putting concrete on a dozen drives in a day, so be it. At least they were still in business.

There was nothing wrong with the original plan. In other circumstances, it might have been a runaway success. But, as we have seen here, circumstances do change. The quicker you are able to recognise that and react to it, the more chance you have of surviving them.

What all this adds up to is a need to:

Regularly review and monitor the plan

This way, you can make a course correction the moment things seem to be going awry. There are a number of ways to do this.

At its simplest level, you should hold a monthly meeting where you assess process against the original plan. Take each of your priorities in turn and identify any areas where improvement or adjustment is needed. Maintain morale by encouraging the team to bring along evidence to show where they are succeeding in bringing this plan alive.

Alternatively, display the team plans online, on a programme that everyone in the team has access to on a daily basis. Bespoke programmes are available from www.upagearperfromance.com. Online programmes display the plans and require the team to regularly interact by scoring how well they are doing in meeting the goals. It will help everyone involved immediately see and understand problem areas and begin the dialogue to make the necessary adjustments.

Once you do this, and everyone is asking the right questions, everyone on the team will own the flexibility. When you have an environment where everyone is constantly thinking and re-evaluating the situation, then you are well on the way to creating a high performing team.

Rigid flexibility raises the chances that whatever is happening will always be responded to effectively.

How rigid flexibility helps us to reach our goals

When the chips are down and things are not going right, rigid flexibility is the way to get through it calmly and efficiently. In short, it always gets a company back on track.

When you see it in action, it can be pretty impressive. One of my clients which had been doing pretty well with its goals was suddenly facing some very unwelcome interference from its regulator. The looming crisis, which was entirely unexpected, threatened to close down 50 per cent of the business. Most businesses would, perhaps understandably, have crumbled at this point. This one didn't. Not one bit.

The team leader could very well have locked himself in his office as he stared in the face the very real possibility that he could both lose his job and be responsible for losing dozens of his staff on his watch too. But, he didn't do that either.

Instead, he gathered everyone together and laid out the situation as he saw it. He explained the legal advice that the firm had been given and the potential outcomes from various scenarios. He reminded everyone that they still had a job to do and goals to meet. Whatever happened with the regulator, the company would go on, in one way or another and it was up to the team to explore the various avenues currently open to them and adjust accordingly.

And, that is exactly what they did. The discussions which followed did not go along the lines of; how are we going to survive this week? It focussed on how they were going to get through the short-term battle and then what they would do to achieve the goals they agreed the year before which were already well on the way to completion. By adopting a stance of rigid flexibility, they dealt with the unexpected crisis, balanced it with the original plan and moved forward like an unstoppable force. If anything, the intervention of the regulator served to stiffen their resolve and make them work together even more effectively.

This was some time ago and as I write I can share with you the outcome. It was not perfect in that some of the redundancies had to take place thanks to the intervention of the regulator, but the lions share of the company survived and eventually thrived. The leader is still in place and acknowledged by the parent company as a safe pair of hands in a crisis.

That is the power of rigid flexibility.

THE PRACTICAL APPROACH to RIGID FLEXIBILITY:

- No plan, however thorough, survives first contact with the outside world.
- Teams have to constantly track performance against their goals, so that they can see immediately when things need adjustment. (Usually the Plan was good- it only needs to be adjusted now)
- Rigid flexibility is a discipline for the whole team – it is not just directed from the top.
- Encourage a culture of being comfortable with constructive challenge.
- To get everyone into the mindset of rigid flexibility, all plans should be regularly 'what iffed'.
- As a leader, work hard to encourage people at every level of the organization to have the courage to take the initiative in the interests of the end game.
- ALWAYS ensure EVERYONE is clear as to the MISSION.
- Rigidly flexible teams have more fun.

Chapter seven - It's not about you and it's all about you

Self Mastery and you – the Team Leader

Whether you are a Team Leader or aspiring to be, this is the area of your life and business which is the difference that makes the difference. Leadership.

I heard a Leadership talk on You Tube that promoted just two elements to be a great leader as follows:

- It is not about you.

And

- It is ALL about you!

This part of the book is 'about you', the other chapters are about how to create the environment in which people align, are inspired and enjoy being mutually supportive. It is about how you cause your people to look forward to their days work and return home fulfilled each and every day.

Keller and Papasan in their book 'The One Thing' state that "you must adopt the mindset of someone seeking Mastery – a commitment to becoming your best.

Most Leaders either silently or otherwise aspire to be really great and the funny thing is that it is always totally possible. What have the following great Leaders got in common?

- Pep Guardiola – twenty four major honours and probably the most successful manager at present in World Football.

- Nelson Mandela – a long winding road to amazing transformational success as a leader.
- Toto Wolff – Successful Business investor, leader of Mercedes Motor Sport the world's best in Formula one and time for family and philanthropy.
- Sir Clive Woodward OBE – England Rugby Coach of the only Northern Hemisphere World Cup winners ever.
- Sir Alex Ferguson – One of the UKs most consistently successful Football Managers.

Study them, they all possess Vision, work and behave consciously to Values, they all pursue the principles of High Performing Teams as espoused in the following pages harnessing the efforts of others into consistent high levels of performance.

You can also do that, you can have their characteristics and change your world when you follow your vision with action.

It may seem obvious that the Team Leader needs to (as Jim Collins Level 5 Leadership positively informs us) get the right people in the right seats on the bus. Also that the Leader needs to inspire a positive Vision of the Future, ensure that Values are Aligned on and behaved, that there is a Plan , a constructive Attitude and room for Rigid Flexibility.

The Leader **also** has to have an open mind to improving her/ his self particularly in the following areas (remember the old adage "what got you to here won't get you to where you want to be!!);

- Emotional intelligence
- Management of / harnessing of their ego

- Willingness / propensity to Coach and Coax
- Learn about themselves in order to model the way they want their High Performing Team to be

This critical Chapter is about you and your responsibility to continue to grow and develop – modeling the way towards enjoying all round high performance for everyone concerned.

> "Managing yourself is the most impactful responsibility you will ever have at any level… AND the only one over which you have full control"

The principal influences for this potentially life changing Chapter are many and include:

- My own bad and occasionally good Leadership experience with the advantage of hindsight.
- Observations whilst Performance / Leadership Coaching hundreds of Teams and Individuals
- Level 5 Leadership – the triumph of humility and fierce resolve as presented by Jim Collins which I have used endlessly whilst Executive Coaching others
- A range of ' mindfulness ' programs participated in since 2004 along with being a daily meditator
- Eckhart Tolle writings – particularly The Power of Now, Stillness Speaks and New Earth
- Jung and studies of 'ego' and 'identity'

MY PLEA TO YOU RIGHT NOW is steal some time to absorb these pages – drop the 'busy' paradigm (my experience of Teams and Individuals is that the " not enough time / too busy ' issue has a variety of root causes like:-

- Not developing your people
- Not trusting your people to do it your way
- Not taking time to demonstrate and Coach
- Sticking with outdated processes
- Not seeing mistakes as a part of people developing

It is NOT that there is not enough time!)

> "True intelligence operates silently. Stillness is where creativity and solutions to problems are found"
>
> Eckhart Tolle

Excellence is not an act – it is a habit.

Self Mastery therefore is a process rather than an end result, it's a mindset .It needs to cover everything from your purpose in life, your vision of the future through to getting started on the right 'stuff' and leading to creating habits of excellence in all the Roles of your life (Leader, Parent, member of your community and so on) for which you have the responsibility to integrate into a valued balance. Self Mastery is as much about 'self leadership' – the Royal Military College Sandhurst moto is 'Serve to Lead' meaning take care of the needs of the task , the team AND the individuals. You do that first, however it will require you to have mastered yourself in order that doing that first comes naturally and consciously.

Effective Leadership of self is the by- product of emotions associated with behaviors such as Self Confidence, Self Reliance, Optimism, and Empathy. How we honestly view ourselves crucially impacts virtually every aspect of your experience. Feeling good about ourselves has to be founded on deep concrete foundations and the two key areas we rely on for that are 'personal confidence' and a genuine feeling of 'self worth'. The process of Self Mastery is fundamentally about building those core personal characteristics. This is a commitment to becoming your 'best' so to achieve extra ordinary you must embrace the extra ordinary that it represents.

Mastery means that you are a master of what you know and an apprentice of what you do not yet know. It is important at this stage to note just a few of the valuable components of emotional intelligence worth working on.

- Optimism being the ability to look on the bright side of life and maintain a positive attitude even in the face of adversity.
- Stress tolerance is the ability to withstand adverse events and stressful situations without falling apart.
- Happiness is the ability to feel satisfied with ones life, to enjoy oneself and others, and to have fun.
- Interpersonal relationship being the ability to establish and maintain mutually satisfying relationships that are characterized by intimacy and by giving and receiving affection.
- Reality testing is the ability to assess the correspondence between what you are experiencing (the subjective) and what in the reality exists (the objective).
- Self actualization being the ability to realize one's potential capacities and to strive to do that which one wants to do.
- Empathy being the ability to stop and put yourself in others shoes thus understanding them as individuals.

These are a powerful group of competencies and when I am Executive Coaching Leaders it is very rare that I find that they are in balance and that there is little to be improved upon. I include myself in this despite the regular reminders I get when Coaching other people. (a good start for the reader will be to self assess score the seven elements above , marks out of ten then ask ten others you work with to do the same. It is rare that we appear to others as we view ourselves!!)

Be aware of your biggest Success Inhibitor

My emphasis of this element of Self Mastery is encouraged by my very own ' ego mismanagement story' and seeing its destructive impacts on 'team performance' in so many team situations with Teams I have worked with over the past 27 years. If ego inhibits true success by preventing a direct and honest connection to the world around us it is because we own the mindset of we are better than we really are! (Just read the last sentence again.)

Whilst this is not a clinical look at ego it is absolutely critical to being on a path towards self mastery, a path to being the very best that you can be that we each grasp or re-grasp the power that the ego has to either build or destroy the positive possibility that surrounds us all.

In all my exposure to Team Leaders and Teams, when I had a Corporate Role and the past 27 years of Coaching Business owners, Senior Executives and Teams THE ONE THING THAT PREVENTS them being the best that they can be is the damage that an inflated ego drive creates. Humility is a rare commodity in today's leaders!

I once had – and often observe in others – a smiling face along with an unhealthy belief in my own importance, a sprinkling of arrogance and self centered ambition. That is **ego.** Sadly, like some of the people I observe today, that produced more than satisfactory bottom line results BUT it could have produced even higher ROI and significantly greater personal growth and role satisfaction for ALL stakeholders. We were not a 'high performing team' by its true definition, just by short term results! We definitely were not the best that we could have been.

Harold Geneen was the CEO of the world's largest ever conglomerate in the 1970's and 80's when he came to London to review the progress of one of his Companies of which I was a Main Board Director .His amiable conversation over lunch following the review was, until several years later when I read the book The Sovereign State of ITT, was lost on me. He compares the state of egoism with alcoholism as follows:

"The egoist does not stumble about knocking things of the desk .He does not stammer or slur. No, instead, he becomes more and more arrogant, and some people, not knowing what is underneath such an attitude, mistake his arrogance for a sense of power and self-confidence."

With success, particularly power, come some of the greatest and most dangerous delusions – entitlement, control and paranoia. Happily I did not suffer from all of that and with hindsight, a courageous career move led me into a more emotional self awareness and greater empathy allowing me to make more of my potential in building my own business. A challenging and humbling journey of 18 years leading through resilience to a rewarding outcome for our clients, our staff and myself.

Self Mastery is a commitment to get yourself more appropriately ready to make the most of yourself BEFORE diving into the task ahead constantly driving for the results the organization or indeed you want. Elsewhere in this book there are guidelines or in some cases much detail on how to consider Purpose (why do you want to do this?)

Vision, Values and Planning. Well as an individual you will only master the best from yourself when you have taken all those elements seriously and created your own Vision and Plan to lead you there over the ensuing three to five years. To build and maintain a cohesive Team FIRST you must build and maintain a cohesive you.

Mastering Team Leadership

Whilst still on ' it is all about you' – you have to gain absolute clarity around 'why does your business and your Team exist', what difference is it making in the world, what your imperative behavioral Values are to be, who will support you in making the behavior changes you will need to make. It is a 'must' to have answers to these questions. They will help you in recruitment decisions, surrounding yourself with people who believe what you believe and want to align behind your inspirational Vision of the future.

> "Find a Coach – you will be hard pressed to find anyone who achieves extraordinary results without one"
>
> G. Keller Author.

Coaching and coaxing , a skill I learned at Sandhurst by probably the very best of instructors there are, is something that many senior executives believe is , as well as 'beneath them' they also believe that they have hired people who should not require to be Coached.! Wrong on both counts.

Even if an individual is not a subject matter expert technically almost all leadership Roles are about harnessing the efforts of others to accomplish bottom line results. People skills ought to be being Coached or polished continuously. The mnemonic that supported me for over 40 years is PESOS – standing for Prepare and Explain why and what the intention is, practice and Show what is expected, Observe the activity together and the feedback and Supervise thereafter. That is how people grow, no matter how important their role or how senior they are.

When you see mastery as a journey to go on instead of the end game you arrive at, it begins to feel attainable and accessible. (Purpose – Vision – Values and Plan are shared in detail within this book for your Team, they are the foundations of your own self mastery too).

The Journey towards Mastery:

There are many many leaders out there producing results which are almost!. Almost satisfactory, almost 100%, would have been better if…. This had happened or that had not happened. They are not leading High Performing Teams, they are doing 'OK' but they are not as outstanding as they could be. Life is 'happening' to these folk, they are not taking full responsibility and accountability for everything that they can control. There are many excuses for not qualifying as a Master and therefore not leading a High Performing Team where fellow leaders are having a ball looking forward to getting to work and going home fulfilled day after day. The most common excuse, the one it seems the majority buy into, is TOO BUSY !!!!

Activity ('busy') is often unrelated to productivity, and busyness rarely takes care of business.

This is what you have to Master on your journey towards true Mastery, the busy paradigm requires a deep courage to address it. We just do not know our limits until we challenge ourselves and keep reaching out for Self Mastery.

A practical daily approach to Self Mastery.

1. Write down what you appreciate from the past 24 hours. (work, health, personal accomplishments, relationships) – this is energizing and lifts the mind towards the art of the possible.
2. Decide what mindset/feeling will be best to support you in the day ahead.
3. Write down the few (3-6) Tasks that must be completed today to move you closer to realizing your business and personal Vision of the future.
4. Remind yourself of particular elements of your Vision that make you smile.

Note: This daily task, as well as your Purpose Vision and Goals must be written down / be in print or they just do not count.

Personal support on your journey towards Self Mastery:

- Share your Plan with those close to you (it is hard to support you if they don't know!).
- Create and adhere to a personal health and fitness regime. (This creates positive energy and stamina).
- I am a great fan of meditation. (It is a means to self awareness, self regulation, and self transformation.) Mindfulness directs the attention of flashlight inward and examines what is and is not working. By illuminating the inner black box, it creates the possibility of abandoning an unwanted behavior. The unwanted behaviors are typically old habits which have got us to where we are today!!)

- Find a Performance Coach for your Team. Managing and Leading the Team is your job. Support from an independent specialist is what Professionals commit to.
- Focus on the heart of things daily – identify the consistent distractions and empower others to take responsibility.
- Give meaning to what you are doing – beyond making money.
- Read Rudyard Kiplings IF every week

Peter Drucker taught me a helpful metaphor: imagine the mind as a raging river and taken for a wild ride by our thoughts and emotions. Take the perspective of sitting on the bank as an impartial spectator. The shift in perceptual stance is critical, fostering the ability to watch your thoughts from an objective position. In essence this what meditating does for us. You are not your thoughts!

Self Mastery is connecting purpose to your current priority, it is you taking full responsibility for your outcomes by holding only yourself responsible and being the author of your results. It is all about you, not about you **and** serving to lead.

Part 2: The four characteristics of a high performing team

Chapter eight - Trust

Very recently, after completing a plane crash team work exercise with aplomb, a client asked me; why do we perform so well on these exercises, yet it never seems to translate into the real, day-to-day reality of the team?

For those of you not familiar with such an exercise, the plane crash simulates a disaster where the entire team has crashed in the jungle. Everyone present has to decide what to leave behind before setting out to find safety. The idea behind this classic group communication and decision-making exercise is to show that, with a little give and take, a group can come to consensus and work successfully for the common good.

The problem is, while it often works beautifully in the sanitized and highly supportive atmosphere of the training room, as soon as everyone gets back to their office, they generally carry on just as before, working in an insular, almost defensive, manner completely failing to utilize the valuable learning from the exercise.

I come across numerous examples of where the Team Leader has identified the area of dysfunctionality in the Team and as they tell me "we have tried this psychometric, and that one and that one, they were really good but the problem is still there!

What does this tell us? Clearly, as my client's teamwork exercise proved, his team had what it takes to perform at a high level with an impressive degree of competence and intent. What is lacking when they get back to the office is trust. Real trust. The sort of deep rooted trust which can take time to build, but when you've got it among a team it is a mind-blowingly powerful force which cannot be broken and resolves issues, and helps everyone make great decisions fast.

For a team to be truly effective, the various members need to know two key pieces of information. They need to know the scale of the task they are tackling and who they are going into battle alongside. Without trust, they will be missing this vital second part.

Why? Because a team founded on distrust or more commonly 'self-serve' is populated by guarded, insular people who are nervous of giving their honest opinion lest it makes them appear foolish or out of place. There is no chance of the conflict, confrontation and honest discussion that are the productive characteristics of a highly effective team because no one will be prepared to let their guard down and will mask their true concerns.

This lack of trust is displayed in many and often seemingly innocent ways. I had an eye-opening demonstration of this when working with one team which felt that there may be some trust issues to resolve. I had set up a very sensitively facilitated exercise to allow everyone to give each other direct feedback as to how they impacted the team's progress. At the end, each person present had to describe behavioural changes they would make to improve the team's culture.

It quickly became obvious that the ego of one member of the team simply could not allow him to describe that he may be anything other than perfect. Although he declared defiantly; "I fully accept all my feedback and I fully commit to achieving 100% of my sales objectives," the subtext was there for all to see.

No one had even mentioned his sales results or indeed discussed any sort of sales activity at all, they had simply pointed to behaviours not conducive to a team result.

This man simply could not trust the team to hear him acknowledge the true weaknesses that had been referred to. He just couldn't bring himself to vocalize them.

This of course was of deep concern to the team leader. Unless the trust issue was addressed – and fast – any challenge or conflict involving this man would only ever end up as adversarial, rather than constructive and productive. His behaviour slowed down decision making.

What this experience proves is; a team that does not trust each other is less honest and less willing to work together. Individuals on that team will avoid any meaningful communications of any kind to protect themselves instead.

That is why you have to work hard to get trust on a team. Without it you will never enjoy the fruits of two plus two equals five or more. The basis for a high performing team is an unconstrained creative involvement from everyone. This requires team members to be fully committed and to do that you need trust.

If not treated carefully and constantly nurtured though, trust within a team can easily be destroyed. It can be broken by a careless slip of a tongue, or by a decision that is badly managed, or by a promise that is not kept. Then, once it is gone, it is very difficult to get back.

Trust is a foundation for a high performing team. There is little point declaring the vision and values and expecting the team to align behind them, unless the trust issue is resolved. People may nod enthusiastically at the plan, but their hearts won't be in it. The team won't be able to give their full commitment because deep down they will be worried and suspicious. The individuals on that team will lack confidence in both their own abilities and in that of the team leader.

There is a distinct and noticeable difference between a team which is trained to do what it is told and follow the plan, and a high performing team where the trust and confidence are genuine. Genuine trust leads to caring mutual support and real vocational satisfaction in a team job well done with everyone's energy aligned.

After all, our most productive relationships are based on trust. Trust is the basis for our drive to contribute.

We need trust because:

With trust, a team can;

- Work together positively to quickly weigh-up and decide on important issues, rather than wasting time on being defensive - wow
- Foster greater understanding of individual roles and how they are linked to others
- Accept that everyone is different – but that is a good thing because everyone can bring distinct strengths to the whole
- Stop wasting time on conforming and self-stereotyping

It is a fundamental human motivation that we are all drawn like moths to a flame to anything that offers us security. However loudly anyone declares they are prepared to do anything to get something done, deep down, we all want to feel well liked, respected, and part of the crowd. What happens? Secretly, everyone is looking around them, mentally calculating what it might take to fit in and be accepted by their colleagues. What are the 'house rules' they will be thinking, so they can fit in, be a 'trusted' member of the team and feel secure?

In most companies, the unwritten house rules are pretty much the same.

Every member of the team should:

- Keep their head down
- Not contribute unless specifically asked to
- Not challenge colleagues, even when it is clear they have made an error
- Shy away from any source of potential conflict
- Continuously make their pitch to show they are on top of their own brief (even if they are not).
- Manage my career whatever the Team outcome might be!

This is not a trusting environment. Everyone may all feel like they are fitting in, but actually they are all being insular and guarded. The result? Innovation is impaired and productivity is slowed down.

In this sort of environment many, many things are talked about, which are never aired when the *whole* team is present. It is the old elephant in the room syndrome – small groups of staff all know about looming problems, but no one is brave enough to mention it when they all get together.

If, on the other hand, there is trust, everyone has the opportunity to address the elephants in the corner of the room. In fact, it is not just 'an opportunity'; they are actively looking for those large grey mammals because they will relish the challenge.

Once the team accepts that everyone is different, but that is OK, it is amazing what they can achieve.

One of the key ways that lack of trust manifests itself is through fear of conflict, which can become a major stumbling block for most teams. I recall one team who were responsible for a multi-million pound turnover organization who had been facing a problem of winning the service contracts which were necessary to keep half of their business in profit. The decline had been steady in recent years and the director responsible for this division was getting increasingly frustrated. He wasn't the only one. There wasn't a team member who wasn't aware of the lack-of-orders elephant in the corner, which was growing larger by the day.

Yet, no one said a thing. Even the chief executive of the whole group couldn't bring himself to bring it out into the open during discussions.

Sound familiar?

To rectify this, I set up a simple exercise to recalibrate what the key result areas were for the next 12 months. I reminded the team that I did not mean goals for divisions, departments, or even individual job roles. This was for the company as a whole. After some discussion we came up with a list of five. I then asked them to identify which one, and only one, did the team require to ensure a breakthrough in the coming 12 months.

Guess what they selected? Yes, service contracts.

Now the subject belonged to everyone. All the team felt responsible, not just the original elephant keeper! Now all the elephants were paraded, it was possible to have an open discussion and brainstorm what needed to happen. Goals were set to ensure a breakthrough in this crucial area and, more importantly, a lesson in trust had been learned by the whole team. Everyone now knew that they were safe getting involved, committed and aligned behind each other's important roles. At last the problem was being addressed.

At a very basic level, when there is trust, productivity goes up. This is because, instead of looking over their shoulder at what everyone else is doing, team members with trust are comfortable in their own skin. They know what their strengths are and are motivated by them. No one will come to a meeting and say; sorry guys, I couldn't get it done after all. They'll have warned everyone weeks before that this might be the case and chances are everyone will have chipped in to make it happen.

Even better though, with trust, they'll know what the strengths and weaknesses of colleagues are because everyone is giving a candid, honest and personal view. This doesn't mean it is open house to mock and belittle them. No. It means that if you are not good at something and a colleague is, then you can openly ask for advice or help. And vice versa. How powerful would that be?

Similarly, conflict will not be a problem. With trust everyone accepts their differences and that we will not always share the same opinions or solutions. But, that is fine. What is important is that everyone is given his or her say and after some discussion the best solution is found. Assertiveness is fine, as long as everyone is aware of the end game and knows their actions will not be misinterpreted as a personal sleight.

With trust, different members of the team will be more disposed to share relevant information. Thus, if one person inadvertently does something which adversely impacts a colleague, an honest conversation can be had, without anyone feeling they have been got at or criticized. Trust enables people to air things which are in the interests of the business in a calm, constructive manner which is to everyone's benefit.

If team members don't have to stop and think about how their comments will be perceived, they will make decisions faster, act quicker and will enjoy what they are doing to the full. They will find it utterly refreshing not to constantly worry about looking or feeling stupid in front of their peers. Hey, this is a great place to work, will be the thought on everyone's minds.

Suddenly all that talk about common vision and values will *really* mean something to everyone.

A team without trust

Is doomed!

Trust is critical in building a high performing team. Show me a dysfunctional team and I will show you one where there is an almost complete lack of trust.

The tell-tale signs of lack of trust are:
- It encourages 'safe' role taking. No one wants to bring up any issues that may show him or her in a weak or vulnerable light.
- Even if the product, service or department is in really bad shape, no one will want to alert the team leader.
- Everyone talks endlessly about the 'great' things

the team accomplishes, even if they are not really relevant to the main picture (or even true at all).

Without trust, no one ever wants to ask the difficult questions, just in case it leads to conflict. Lack of trust causes people to suspect the motives of anyone, and everyone, who questions or comments on something that is not quite right. Thus, something that might seem a mundane operational issue to most people, becomes a personal matter to the members of the team associated with it. They become defensive, distant and confused if anyone has the temerity to question their patch.

Similarly, even if no one flags it up first, no one feels comfortable enough to acknowledge that all is not well in their department. On a team without trust, even if someone knows that they are almost certain to miss an important deadline, you can bet that they won't say a word until they no longer have a choice. The result? Chaos, disappointment and general acceptance of low standards of delivery.

How much better would it have been if weeks earlier this person would have felt comfortable enough to say; guys I am going to need some help if we are going to get X finished in time? It wouldn't just have been better for our paranoid friend.

It would have been better for the *whole team.*

It is always very apparent when a team is ridden with mistrust. Talk to individual members on a one to one basis and they'll be most eager to tell you what an important operator they are. They'll give numerous examples of their successes and maybe even boast about their bonuses or remuneration. Press them further though, and ask about their colleagues and you'll probably get a roll of the eyes. The dismissive stance may be backed with an anecdote about how a team-mate fluffed a meeting, or held up a vital project, or just isn't up to the job. You could not get a better demonstration that this person is only interested in their own silo and is in a team that completely lacks any sort of trust or mutual respect.

Do you think our well-paid team member would ever open up if he or she was struggling with a project? Not a chance. They'd rather go home every night tearing out their hair out with worry and stress.

And that disastrous project? No one will ever know it was going off the rails until it is too late to do anything about it.

How different it would have been if there was trust and cooperation in team.

The credibility gap

I once worked with a team at a major bank who were doing pretty well, but something was not quite right. The team leader assured me everyone got on well and seemed to be pulling in the right direction. In fact, he added, he had recently recruited a real star. This guy had been brought in to mastermind an important project and had shone from the start. He was clearly intellectually very bright and had got to know the ropes really quickly. In fact, he had really got to the heart of the issue he was trying to solve.

The only problem was, he didn't seem to rate his new team-mates much and was constantly trying to undermine their credibility. If something didn't go to plan, he was all too willing to go to his new boss and point the finger of blame.

"What am I to do?" said the team leader. "This guy is really bringing in the results, but he is challenging operations at every turn. It is really starting to undermine the whole operation because no one is immune from his criticism."

This problem is not as uncommon as you might think. Unfortunately it makes any trust issues a lot, lot worse. Believe it or not, this bright young fellow is the worst sort of internal terrorist you can get.

Most people assume that internal terrorists are incompetent. They are usually not. In fact, it is because this fellow is so competent and bringing in the results that he can get away with being such an effective internal terrorist.

If someone is bringing in top results every month, no one can question their competence. If the competence goes unchallenged, so does the credibility.

This has got to stop. People like our friend here undermine the trust and the confidence of the whole team. Just because they get results, it does not mean that they are a credible, or irreplaceable team member.

I would think very carefully about whether people like this have a place on your team. The damage they can do to trust is brutal and long lasting. Plus, in the long-term, the productivity gains from a high performing, trusting team, will far outweigh the efforts of any so-called individual star. Yes, they may be handy to have around, but not if they ruin all your good work.

Remember, even if a player is recognised as 'great', if he or she is undermining the confidence of everyone else, then you haven't got a great team.

Trust is…

Both active and passive

Active is all about confidence in the leadership of the team, in veracity and in reliable communications. Active trust is driven by big emotions.

A passive feeling of trust is the absence of worry and suspicion about being let down or betrayed.

If you want to know when you have 'made it' as a high performing team, it is when the trust among the members is passive. You have created such a great environment to work in that trust is no longer an issue, it is a part of the culture. Anyone can say and do anything, and know that they will always be supported. Meanwhile, everyone else will be constantly jumping in with new ideas.

Doesn't that sound like an enticing prospect?

Creating trust

There is no complex formula to create trust within teams. No step-by-step rules, or lengthy training course, or clever questionnaires (well there is one-Covey Speed of Trust (see appendix). All you need is open, honest, brave common sense.

Successful trust building hinges on communication and the team leader needs to model the way – suspend judgemental thoughts, request and expect the best of and in others and you will attract a trusting environment.

Prepare

Assure the team, you are not playing the blame game. This is not a witch-hunt, but the beginning of a new era.

Get a feel for the barriers to trust. Encourage individual team members to talk openly about their own frustrations and misunderstandings from their own perspective. Ask them; have they felt blocked, or excluded, or belittled?

Then, work with them to dig a little deeper. How have they been dealing with these problems thus far? Are they in denial and just ignoring things while the problem festers? Are they pretending to all and sundry that it really doesn't matter, while secretly feeling more and more stressed about it every day?

In an ideal world, what would they do instead? Listening to understand is a great skill to practice here.

Listen

Successful conversations to promote trust take hard work from both sides. If the leader knows people are holding back, he has to elicit a willingness from them to listen and to encourage them to open up. It can be a tough call because senior executives don't like admitting they need help.

Then, just as importantly, the leader has to ensure that he or she does not respond in a way that causes their teams to go back into their shell again.

To listen well, the questioner has to separate the act of *receiving* information from the act of *judging* information. That means, when a team member is encouraged to speak frankly, the response is considered and non-assumptive. Abrupt interruptions, restlessness, or even a frown on behalf of the listener will render the whole exercise useless. If the leader reacts badly, even if only through his or her body language, the trust issue will just become more difficult.

Active listening will make this process easier. Take, for example, a team where certain individuals are continually late to meetings wasting the time of all their more organised colleagues. Leave aside the obvious reaction which is to finally snap and yell; we really have to put paid to this habit of always starting meetings late! Instead, consider the power of the following response;

Has anyone got any suggestions as to how we could be more efficient in our time keeping so that we can all use each other's time to the best effect?

I know which approach would get me speaking up and contributing to a constructive resolution.

The leader has to demonstrate through careful listening that anyone having a weakness in their game is simply something everyone needs to know about so that we can support. It will not, however, generate any negative views about that person in the future. Therefore the person at the top has to create an environment where it is OK to talk about anything and everything openly and frankly.

Move forward – together

Once you know what the barriers are, it is time to convert them into a winning attitude. Communicate very clearly what you would like the modus operandi of the team to be. Frame the action, clarify the responsibilities and accountabilities and then offer everyone your full support.

Explain to the team that if there is an enemy, that enemy is not within the team. That enemy is outside of the company and if the team wants to defeat it all they have to do is work together. And keep on working together.

Trust is like the rest of the cogs in a high performing team. It needs oiling and working on *all* of the time. Keep a constant eye out for instances when people have been brave, and praise them. Constantly reinforce the good behaviour. Similarly, when a colleague appears to be worried about this or that, or don't think they can complete something, ask if they need help. Slipped commitments don't mean false commitments; there could be good reasons why this team member is struggling. If a team leader is not accusatory, but listens carefully and corrects the issue collaboratively, it sets the tone for the whole team.

So, in short, to create a high performing team based on trust a leader must:

- Demonstrate openness and a supportive environment consistently (do not save it for a half year appraisal!)
- Use feedback fast - or lose the opportunity.
- Listen intently.
- Demonstrate respect for every member of the team and encourage them to do the same for each other.
- Remove any sense of threat.
- Make sure everyone contributes. All the time. Every day.

Taking ownership

It is all very well listening, creating an open atmosphere, encouraging everyone to speak up and not shy away from conflict. Yet, it can all still, quite easily, fall apart. Why? Because:

Trust is a two way process.

Let's not forget, leaders are human too. They are subject to the same insecurities and fears as their subordinates, however well they have learned to hide them over the years.

Self-trust is a vital part of the trust pyramid. The team leader has to accept that they themselves have weaknesses. That's OK. We all do. Yes, if you are in a position of power and responsibility it can be a tough call to admit that you are worried about not getting something done when all eyes are on you, but that is what it takes if you want a real atmosphere of trust.

The team leader has to be just as willing to open up to his or her subordinates as he or she expects them to be in return. Without doing so, it is impossible to move on to the next level. After all, if you don't accept your own fallibility, how can you ever hope to resolve issues among the team? Practicing what you preach is vital, or everything you have done to promote trust within the team will have been a complete waste of time.

A global organisation once engaged me to work with its recently reorganised top team in the UK. The new CEO there was a bright, engaging person who was very clear about what he wanted.

He was particularly clear as to his long-term vision. Yet, when I met individually with members of the team, not one of them seemed to know what this vision was.

What was going wrong? I probed a bit deeper and discovered that this CEO was in the habit of regularly sending one line emails to various members of the team commenting on something he had just observed, or challenging something which didn't seem to fit in with the bigger picture. This has the impact of 'micro managing' and creating a feeling among the team of having their competence challenged.

The team on the receiving end of these missives, also often found them irrelevant or confusing. Misunderstanding his motives, they began to mistrust the leader. Instead, they subconsciously resolved to look after themselves.

So, I set out to discover what was behind these brief emails. I didn't need to look much further than the CEO's bulging inbox, which had 180 unread emails awaiting his attention. 'And this is a quiet day,' he joked. But this was a serious matter.

His response to the weight of communication was to blast out numerous pithy emails to show he was 'dealing with things'. The trouble is, these emails weren't helping anyone and simultaneously destroying trust among the team. Meanwhile, the CEO was constantly agitated that he did not have the time to communicate his vision.

What this man had inadvertently done was to create a self-preservation culture of low trust. Needless to say, the first thing I did with this company was to clarify the vision fast and also started a journey to significantly reduce the amount of emails the CEO felt obliged to respond to.

Team leaders must recognise that there is an important link here with purpose and attitude too. To have a high performing team, an important part of a leader's purpose is that they put a high value on trust. Enjoying being in trusting and professional relationships should be a statement that is near the top of their list, if not at the top.

Too many leaders don't even consider trust has a place in their professional relationships. Yes, trust comes into their home and social life, team leaders are often just as guilty as their subordinates for thinking that trust between colleagues just doesn't seem to come into the equation just as long as everyone 'gets along'. But, basing working relationships on a trust/friendship basis makes the situation vulnerable on both sides. No, what a team leader should be aiming for is the professional trusting relationship outlined here.

Trust in professional relationships is the key to getting things done.

Ditch the limiting mind-sets

Why does a kid not ask, or challenge, a question in class? It is because, sometime in the past, someone made a fool of him once when he asked a challenging question. It may have been a fellow pupil, or even a teacher, but the result is the same.

When he becomes an adult, this same person may get chewed by his boss for a perceived misdemeanour. The result? He will keep his head down, not ask any questions and stick to the bare minimum, bare bones, of his job description forever more.

Throughout our careers, we have each, unknowingly picked up a set of beliefs and opinions from experiences. These beliefs are formed via both facts and assumptions, but both are equally powerful forces.

Some of our beliefs are positive, where something has worked well, so you will do it again and again. At the other end of the scale, are experiences akin to our once inquisitive school kid, where something has unexpectedly blown up in your face and ensured you never, ever try that again. A feeling of shock, anger, fear and loss fuels that feeling of 'never again'. Subconsciously it reduces your motivation to go the extra mile, or to be flexible to new ideas, or take appropriate risks.

That 'never again' feeling has a profound effect on trust. If an individual believes they have been disappointed before in a similar situation, chances are they will shy away from the current scenario. If they have been let down by one boss, they may automatically conclude that all bosses are the same. Just telling someone; no, no, this time is different, will inevitably, perhaps understandably, be met with scepticism.

It would be a huge mistake to underestimate the damage caused by these limiting mindsets. It affects everyone on every level.

Individual team members who harbour the blind spots will find it impossible to open up. It will seriously hamper their ability to grow and develop.

Meanwhile, team leaders will be fighting numerous hidden barriers to trust among all the individuals on their team. It's not made any easier by the fact that each team member has differing blind spots based on their own past experiences.

This is why it takes time, perseverance and vigilance to build up trust. It won't happen overnight. It is not a fast or easy process to get people into a position where they won't be embarrassed to say, detail isn't my forte, can you give me a hand? Or, I have always had a problem with public speaking; can you help me on this important presentation?

But, by constant active listening and leading by example it is possible.

Imagine though the power if people felt able to open up and banish the ghosts of their past?

If you knew that no one was out to undermine you if you admit your weakness, do you think you'd shuffle along as before? Or, do you think you'd set yourself some big, hairy arsed goals, to show everyone just how indomitable your strengths are?

How trust helps us reach our goals

As I have said many times in this book; 'no plan survives contact with the enemy' and as many businesspeople will attest, the same can be said of corporate life. Even the best thought-out strategies need refinement, or even a complete rethink, once they are brought out into the real world.

It is because of this, perhaps above all else, that trust is so important in a high performing team. Things will go wrong. Plans will change. Life won't be a smooth ride. But, when there is trust in the team, it won't be an issue.

With trust in the team, if there is a big issue and all hands are needed on deck, no one will be moaning about it. Or making excuses. Or saying it is not their problem. In fact they won't be saying anything. They'll have already just rolled up their sleeves to get on with it.

That is what trust does.

Everyone will trust the leader's judgement that the issue at hand is more important than what they are currently doing. They will trust that a member of the team needs help because something isn't happening. They will respond without question.

I was working recently with an organisation who had just completed a relocation from several sites to the one and in doing so effected cost savings through a redundancy programme. There was low trust on the Executive Team and the HR Director was complaining to me that it ought not to have been their responsibility to organise and facilitate an 'all organisation' meeting. The complaint was born of fear of the event not going well and her not being supported by her peers. On a high performing team this would have been viewed as a brilliant and exciting opportunity and responsibility, something everyone would want to be involved in and be a part of. I could understand the stress upon the HR Director but after working on trust issues in the team, I am pleased to report that I heard that the meeting went very well indeed.

The key points to understand about Trust are:

- Recognise the power of credibility in that it involves integrity, intention and ability as well as results
- Leader has to encourage and sustain an open and honest environment always aligned on the end game, the vision
- Model the way through constructive challenges, as well as open appreciation and recognition of what is being done well in the organisation
- Model the behaviour expected of people everywhere in the team and organisation
- Constantly be openly sharing the vision and how you may be innovative in reaching it

HELP people realise that Team before Self will build a better personal career profile than self first

Chapter nine - Passion

In recent years, organisations have been forced to ruthlessly reign in costs in response to the tough business environment. No one knows what Brexit and post Brexit might bring – all we know from history however is that with change comes opportunity. Many businesses have had at least two cracks at cutting back on staff. Some have gone even further and, in a series of painful moves, have cut down their workforce to the bare minimum. What this meant was that after the first round of redundancies many employees were left with having to do 10 to 20 per cent more work to fill in the gaps. After the second round, a further 10 to 20 per cent was added on to their workload. Impossible though it might seem, some poor souls are struggling to do considerably more than this. It is not a comfortable situation for anyone involved. It also seems unlikely that most businesses will be improving this situation any time soon by recruiting more bodies to ease the workload. Indeed, after the shocks of the credit crunch, they may well never do so. I was recently extending my practice of meditation / mindfulness and attending a programme along with several others. I was saddened that such a high percentage of my fellow participants purpose in taking the course was to be better able to handle the pressure of workload/ stress in their workplaces.

There is, however, an answer to easing the pressure on those left behind. It lies in a business model which would enable firms to get more out of their teams, even if they have been substantially reduced in number. This model does not involve anyone being put under more pressure, or being made to work even longer hours. If anything, it will considerably reduce the burden on all concerned. If that sounds like an enticing and inspiring prospect it is because it is.

Relieving the load and improving the prospects and moral of your put-upon workforce can be achieved by finding the *passion* in your team, finding the ability to focus, to decide and to act with energy.

Passion is the bedrock of the calculation where $4 + 4 = 5$ or more. Ignite the fire that will drive a team on to high performance status and things will become easier. Considerably so.

Passion is a key component of a high performing team because you can't win at anything unless you are truly and unequivocally passionate about it. Someone once said; 'It's not enough to aim, you have to hit'. When passion exists, then hitting the target becomes the norm. Passion creates 100 per cent commitment and a cycle of positive thought becomes a self-fulfilling prophecy. It is a fact that leaders looking for the positive attract more that is positive. This, in turn means they enjoy their role more and as a result become a role model of positive reinforcement. It is that simple, you can choose!

Oh, and, in case you were thinking the answer lies in putting on a cheery disposition and handing out a few jolly high fives to get this side of things sorted, don't. Passion has to be genuine.

A senior manager once confessed to me that he had been faking his passion at work for years. He didn't like the company, thought the strategy wouldn't work and his boss was an idiot. However, he had a mortgage to pay, school fees to settle and liked to indulge his passion for collecting vintage cars. So, year after year, he smiled, made encouraging noises, got on with his job and collected the pay cheque.

Do you think his lack of conviction made a difference? You bet it did. Aside from the fact that it is actually quite stressful to an individual to go on pretending that he or she is passionate about something when they are not, and to be constantly on their guard about saying something they shouldn't, it does have an effect on the rest of the team. The senior manager may have had the acting skills of Laurence Olivier (he didn't) but however convincing people are at trying to appear passionate, if they are not, it always leaks out. Somehow, even if it is only something which niggles away in their subconscious, his colleagues will pick up on the duplicity and it will make them feel confused, uncertain and anxious.

With passion, everyone has to be on board. If it turns out that one member of the team is not passionately committed to the strategy, a team is in real trouble. But, if it is the leader who is not convinced, that team is doomed to not realising its full potential or enjoying the journey.

As with so many elements of a high performing team, passion most definitely starts at the top. If the team leader does not have passion, there is no chance whatsoever of creating a high performing team. A high performing team does, after all, start with a high performing leader.

Let's just define what I mean and don't mean by passion here. Passion is about deep reason and direction towards Vision. For a Team to become and sustain High Performance its 'passion' needs to be deliberate, have clarity, and a methodological determination. What we are not talking about is 'being the biggest.... Being the most innovative.... Being the best or first ...!'

We need passion because:

Without passion, you won't ever become a high performing team.

The law of attraction teaches us that when something is not as it should be, the faster you are able to turn your attention in the direction of a solution, the better, because wasting time on a continuing exploration of the problem will simply prevent you finding the solution. Having a passion for something causes the 'pull' towards the positive and finding the best solution. Passion is attractive and it acts as a magnet attracting the things you want towards you. The clearer you are about what you want, rather than what you don't want, the more power you will have and the more likely you are to develop a passion for it.

We each possess the qualities of thinking positively, expecting the best in others, of doing what we know in our heart to be the very best thing to do in any given situation. We all have that massive potential and it is often close to the surface and ready for use. Our life journey, role models and experiences may have dampened the positivity in some, but we all have the resource that is the key to unlocking the principles of high performing teams.

The key is to ignite the passion for what we want and without a doubt, the team leader has the most important part to play in this journey. And more scientific (this is a Sales and Marketing man writing!!) – it is less impetuousness and much more discipline, perseverance, strength and mastery.

The opportunities of the future will rarely be obvious – they are more likely to be things we have not seen before, things we are more likely to reject than become passionate about. Our definition of Passion is less 'marketing'

In my experience of working with teams which have really excelled and made their whole a great deal better than the sum of the parts, the common denominator is the leader's passion for having individual team members excel their previous levels of performance and amaze themselves with what they can achieve.

Perhaps you will recall the introduction to this book when I outlined the importance of the team leader and how if she or he has fully bought into the challenge of building a high performing team it can raise the results by 25 per cent? Well, this is the time that figure really comes into play. The quality that underpins this impressive leap in performance, more than any other discussed in this book, is passion.

If a team leader has any hope of transforming 4+4 into 5, 10, 15 or more, they have to passionately believe in what they are doing. The emphasis here is on substance, on functionality, on being prepared to pay a price and on action. It is about discipline, strength and purpose, perseverance and self mastery. Passion releases the energy the person leading a team needs to think and act positively. This, in turn, will lead to a persistent pursuit of the team goals which will realise the results and outcomes that they seek.

The challenge for the team leader is to evolve their own passion and work at igniting the flame in others.

You may think this an obvious requirement for anyone charged with leading a team. But, it is not always so. I have met quite a few leaders who appear to think they can somehow subcontract the passion component. They feel that if they initiate and authorize a team performance programme they are now free to carry on in their own sweet way without them personally having to change. Yet, without a doubt, the individual is where the high performing team starts.

In every genuinely high performing team I have ever worked with, the passion of the leader shines through. It enables him or her to keep the visions and values on the agenda every day, police open and honest communication, constantly clarify two way expectations and be perpetually visible and accessible. Passion gets things done; enjoyably.

Once that passion is felt throughout the team that is when they become a very powerful force indeed.

Passion is not….

Just a word – or a catch phrase on a mug in the staff breakout area.

Passion is a term that is bandied about a lot in businesses. It is probably less commonly used in the UK than the USA, but it is still gradually creeping into every-day corporate speak pretty much everywhere. Executives will tell you that they are 'passionate' about a brand of whisky, or a new electronic gadget, or whatever widget they are flogging right then. What does this really mean? Clearly not a lot because next year they will declare equal fervour to whatever new product is lining up to replace last year's model.

This is not real passion. It is temporary, it is often frantic and impetuous.

You only have to look at two people with the same qualifications and experience to know the difference real passion can make. Leadership is not all about what is on your CV, or charisma, or being able to talk a good game. It is about whether or not you truly believe in what you are doing. Passionate leaders are down to earth, realistic, innovative and creative. They are all of these things because they have the energy and belief that make them so and they are ready to pay the price of perseverance to actually deliver.

They don't ever have to tell you that they are passionate about anything. They just get on with making it happen.

Passion is….

REAL

A leader cannot 'fake' passion to gee up the rest of the team. There is no point talking up a disastrous, or even uninspiring, strategy and telling everyone how good it will be. If you don't really believe in it, the rest of the team will see through you like a shot. They'll dismiss your stirring pep talk as another piece of management rhetoric and after a while will reject pretty much everything that their team leader says.

To go back to the rugby analogy I have touched upon a few times in this book, there is little point a team leader getting everyone in a huddle and giving them a rousing talk before a game. If the inspiration does not come from inside and is not founded on a deep belief that this is the right thing and that we have prepared diligently for this event, it will be just words. No one will truly believe them and will have forgotten them by the time they get out on the pitch. It can't just be high fives and bold words. There has to be real substance.

Yes, that faking leader may keep their job, but because they are not being true to themselves (or their team) they will never, ever reap the benefits and joy of creating a high performing team. They won't be able to bring out the best in those around them and realise the true potential of the team.

However, if the team leader believes, really believes, in what he or she is saying then those around them will know that they are really going to get their place singing.

Passion is a belief. If you passionately believe something, it gives you nerves of steel. Whatever the day throws at you, you will always know that you are doing the right thing and that you are on the right course.

As well as being real, that passion must also be directed towards the right thing. We are all passionate about something, but if you want a high performing team, it must be driven by passion for the goals ahead. If the leader or team is distracted by other passions, their energy will be expended elsewhere to the detriment of all concerned. They will become a roadblock to progress.

I know first-hand what it is like to be the roadblock to releasing the power of passion.

Back in the days when I was a board director of a large financial services firm, I thought I was pretty passionate about my job. I fervently believed that my way was the only way and it helped that I really seemed to be getting results. We were seeing growth of 25 per cent a year, every year, so I felt pretty invincible. I didn't stop to think whether I was passionate about the *right* things though, or whether my passion was just based on what I wanted to achieve, or on what was best for the company.

What I didn't know at the time, because I was not really listening, was that there were some limiting mindsets among my team. They thought; this can't go on. We cannot sustain this level of growth. There does not seem to be a credible long-term strategy. They were right.

I was concentrating my passion onto my own short-term goals. I had not directed my energies to the long-term benefit of my company, or my team.

Although there was not a better way of running that sales force in the moment because we were undoubtedly successful, I should have looked beyond my personal short-term passion, towards the future of the team and the company as a whole.

Sure enough, shortly after I left, sales did plummet and there was a need to change strategy fast. Fortunately, the chief executive at that time had long-term passion. He believed that there was a better way for the company and used his energies to change the entire structure of the organisation. He branched out from insurance and moved into areas like bancassurance, estate agency and financial advice. At the time, this was exactly what this business needed to grow and his strategy energised the whole team.

Finding your passion

Post credit crunch I was called in to work with a team at a large insurance company which mainly worked in the business-to-business arena. It was a small team, struggling with finding a credible business model in an industry that has been hard hit by the downturn. They found that the period taken between meeting new prospects and then them signing on the dotted line was lengthening all the time. Once they would meet a prospective client and be asked; how many days till we can get started? Now, it could take as long as 18 months before any cash started to come in.

The two key issues facing the team leader, who was also managing director in this subsidiary, were:

- How do we speed up the process?
- How do I get my team to think about the bigger picture so they too can come back with ideas on a new strategy?

Yet, after months of grappling with the problem, nothing much seemed to be changing which is why the MD invited me in.

"We don't seem to be making any progress," he complained. "I can't understand what the problem is."

After taking time to listen to the team and the MD, the problem seemed glaringly obvious to me. The man at the top was lacking an essential ingredient to drive this team into high performance status. He lacked passion he looked concerned, not excited.

On the surface, it all looked fine. This fellow had been with the company for 16-years in various positions. The firm had rewarded his loyalty by sending him off on various courses and even gave him time off to do an MBA at one of the large American business schools. The MD had reciprocated by continuing his allegiance to the firm and clearly had a high degree of trust that this mutually beneficial relationship would continue for some time to come.

But, despite all of this, the man clearly didn't have a fire in his belly that said; 'we are going to change all this and make it work.' Why not? Well, ironically, it is for much the same reason that he has been such a valuable employee. He had quite simply been there too long. Over the years he had become so immersed in the engine room of the company culture that he now found it very hard to see how to make a big difference. His passion had become dulled by familiarity. It is the same for anyone who has been in such a position for any length of time. Being there, year in and year out, having to produce a profit time after time, can make it very hard to sustain any passion.

What I had to do was to help this MD see that, like it or not, the passion did have to come from him. He had to find his own passion, before he could ignite that of his team.

The way for this man, indeed any team leader, to find their passion is to get in touch with their purpose by asking themselves three questions:

- What do you like about yourself?
- How do you most like spending your time?
- What would the perfect world be for you?

I'm prepared to put money on the fact that most readers of this book will never have thought about what it is about themselves that they like, let alone written it down. But, until you do, how can you know what makes you tick? Once you do give some thought to what it is that makes your chest expand with joy, it can be quite telling.

Answering these three questions will tell you at a glance if you are passionate about what you are doing in your corporate life. If your work does not even figure on your list, or it shows very clearly that you are not waking up each day feeling joyful about the challenges in the day ahead, then you may need to rethink what you are doing. Here is the question for you to be answering in order to discover a practical purpose – " For the sake of what, am I living the remainder of my life? ". This particular Executive eventually answered creating and delivering a Strategy of real value to the organisation and the staff.`

You may get satisfaction from cutting the lawn, or growing vegetables, playing squash or going to the gym, but they may not be your passions. Personally I love looking at, walking up and being in the Scottish mountains. That is a passion and has been for many years. As a result of it being a passion I am there permanently. I wallow in pride and adoration when I observe my children with each other, their families and other adults. My chest expands when I observe teams having challenging productive discussions where previously there was silence. I have a passion for being the grit in their oyster of ensuring that happens.

How would this question help and guide my MD though? Well, it is an important first step in recognizing the WIIFM (what's in it for me) and what makes him tick. It is also a vital precursor in showing the benefits of *creating* a passion for something. If he took time to create a business model he truly believed in, then it would be easy to find a passion for amazing results through harnessing the efforts of other people. That is what he did - he created, led and implemented that Strategy.

Until you find a business model that will inspire you, you will never be passionate. And, until you find that passion, you will never be able to pass that passion on to your team.

If the answers to those three questions earlier on are all negative, one of the ingredients of a high performing team will be missing. It is a crucial ingredient. If you don't have an absolute passion for what you are trying to achieve in the work place, there is no way you will get the best out of your team. So, now is the time to do something about it.

Another great test of passion is to ask yourself; what is inspiring you at the moment? I remember one of my clients stopping in his tracks – literally – when I asked him this question. I had been coaching him for a while and he always seemed in a tearing hurry to be somewhere else and never quite focused on what he was trying to do with his blue chip business-to-business firm. On the morning in question, we had to squeeze in a meeting at 7.15 am, so he could catch a 9.15 train to his next meeting. I ended up walking to the station beside him to finish the session.

"What's inspiring you at the moment?" I asked as we walked briskly along.

He immediately stopped walking in an effort to give this question his full attention. It was clearly something that troubled him. All our previous discussions that day had been about the problems he had with this major business customer, or niggles with two or three members of the team he led and his desire to get a better rapport/relationship with his Global CEO. Before I asked this important question, he had been focussed on trying to get answers to all these really crucial things.

Finally, he said; "My boys and the under-11 cricket team."

It turned out what made this man tick was his work coaching his sons' cricket team. All his joy, energy and passion was derived from their burgeoning success on the cricket pitch.

None of this means that he was not fully committed to getting the most out of his team, because he quite clearly was. What he didn't have though, was passion for his work at that time.

As I have already said, there can be no high performing team without passion. So, is this guy stuffed in his ambitions? Not a bit of it. What he needed to learn – and indeed did go on to do – is how to transfer the energy he was experiencing on that cricket pitch into what he is doing in the office. It is possible to do and for him to get just as much satisfaction out of the day job.

Learning passion

Passion can be 'learned'. In both of the cases above, the super-busy, cricket loving team leader and the MD of the insurance business clearly did not feel that fire in the pit of their stomachs about the way things were going in the office. However, they both had the opportunity to challenge themselves to create a direction *they could* feel passionate about which would create a more meaningful purpose.

To do this, both of these team leaders needed to get into a position where they could see their businesses differently. They needed to use their considerable intellect and knowledge to find a different way of running their business to kindle that flame; a fresh inspiring Vision in the longer term, and a detailed Strategy of how to get there.

Once they achieved this, and found their passion, they would be able to galvanise their people's innovation and creativity to achieve the goals they really believed in.

The key to learning to be passionate is to create a business model that will inspire you.

Earlier on in this book, we looked at the example of a building company which decided to explore the options of branching out into wind farms. This could have been just the catalyst this team needed to get excited about what could be achieved. The leader of that team and his colleagues may never even have considered this avenue before, but once the seed was planted as part of the long-term plan and began to germinate, the change will be electric. (excuse the pun!) Here is something that everyone could get behind because they will see that it will take them into a new, and potentially highly lucrative, direction.

Setting off on an intellectual investigation of the way to move forward is often all it takes to get everyone champing at the bit. It gives them a concrete belief that they have found something and will inspire and enthuse everyone that there is a better way. Once you believe that this *is* the way to a better future, it is a great feeling indeed.

Think of anything you are currently passionate about. How does it make you feel? It makes you feel energised and eager to pursue this passion again and again. I didn't try snow skiing until I was in my thirties, but once I had given it a go and learned through experience that it was fantastic, I couldn't get enough of this amazing sport. I had learned something intellectually that had touched me internally. We can all do this in our business life. If we can find the vision and goals that inspire us, passion will ensue.

Passing on the passion

If the team leader is passionate about the goal ahead, and it is clearly the goal which will get this company really motoring, the team will be infected by that passion. It works by osmosis. Those around the leader will see what that passion is doing for their leader and that energy is infectious - the Team will proactively want to contribute their efforts towards what the Leader wants.

Of course, the team leader needs to vocalise this passion too. He or she must make sure they share that great strategy and their belief that it is going to work. They must constantly reinforce it too. But, the real power comes from that leader's inner sense of belief in the great journey they are all undertaking.

There is always a chance that someone on the team won't be infected by the passion. There could be many reasons for this, but I would encourage any team leader to use the techniques they used to find their own passion to find that feeling in a reluctant colleague. Ask them those three questions. Find out what makes them tick and then develop things from there.

Don't go in there all guns blazing and accuse them of being a non-believer and drinking from your catch phrase mug! That is just going to make a bad situation worse. No, adopt a coaching relationship and ask them the right questions to find out what makes them feel good. Then work on that to align them with your goals for the team as a whole.

The most important first step is opening up that dialogue so the team member does not feel that they are part of a command and control relationship, but that the leader has a genuine interest in making things better. Once they can be helped to see that they are part of the bigger picture, and can really feel that passion, things will begin to happen.

Very early on in a project to coach a team in Scotland, I saw this in action. On our second review the sales director piped up and said that he really didn't want to say something because it sounded sycophantic, but he also felt duty bound to speak up.

"Go ahead," I said.

"We've really moved on since you've been here," he said.

"You've heard the conversation in the room this morning and can see that we are all being much more open."

"Yes," I replied. "But I haven't given you all that. You all had that before I came here. All I have done is create an environment for you to be more open and honest with each other than you were before."

The fantastic thing about this interchange was that suddenly, because this fellow had spoken out, the belief among the team about the potential it had soared. Now they were united in their passion for what they could achieve, the sky really was the limit.

You don't go on a course to 'learn' passion. It evolves. The best thing a team leader can do is find their own passion and then put together certain elements to convey it to their team. The next step is add a little heat to formulate that steel, fire-up that passion and release the potential.

How passion helps us to reach our goals

As an ardent rugby fan, one of my most proudest achievements was a brief spell working with Sir Clive Woodward, who was manager of the England team from 1997 to 2004, managing them to victory in the 2003 Rugby World Cup, the first northern hemisphere Team to achieve this . Although I was there to advise on leadership team strategies, I confess that I myself learned an awful lot through the experience.

The one thing I learned most from Sir Clive, was the power of passion because he really was a true believer in what his leadership team could do. Don't forget, when he joined the team, the general mind set was that rugby world cups are only ever won by teams from the southern hemisphere. He *knew* differently and of course went on to prove it in spectacular fashion. He paid attention to detail, worked tirelessly to build the best, was not afraid to take risk and innovate.

Sir Clive was brimming with literally 1000s of ideas about how to lead his team to victory. Some of them didn't work, but many of them did. The important point is that he always knew he was going to find something and he did – his passion was powerful as well as infectious.

In many ways he was working from an entirely different business model from the rest of us mere mortals. After all, the difference between a squad which lifts the cup and one which goes empty handed, is often very little performance and fitness-wise. The smallest things can make all the difference. In the corporate world, the variations between the tools most team leaders get to work with can be enormous. But, even though the smallest things made all the difference in Sir Clive's case, his passion gave him the energy to keep on trying until he found that elusive X factor which made his team victorious. We could all learn something from this.

Teams often need to make more fundamental changes in order to 'win' in whichever sector they are in. But, one of the most important elements is the genuineness of the team leader's commitment towards what they are doing and why they are doing it.

That team leader is not doing it because they want to maximise their bonus for the year. That is a given. They are doing it because they can see that there is a bigger opportunity here, not just for them, but for everybody on the team. That is what team work in a high performing team is about. Getting the most out of everybody so 4+4=5, 10, or 15 or more.

Passion is a significant contributor to that difference.

The key points to take from passion are:

- To make the most of any situation, passion has to be one of the early ingredients
- Passion is a mindset – it has to be genuine
- Having passion in the culture is predominantly the responsibility of leadership
- Surely making this a high performing team, which everyone wants to be a part of, is worth getting passionate about?
- False Passion masks weakness
- True Passion of value, is discipline, clarity, strength, purpose and perseverence

---

Chapter ten - Creativity

There was a time when you did not have to be creative to be successful. If you wanted to grow, or fend off a new competitor, or deal with some other looming threat in the marketplace, you simply did more of what you already did. But better. Or faster. Or with a better margin. That is certainly what corporate life in the 1970s and 80s was like.

Thus, for example, if you were a catalogue company, you'd buy a bigger mailing list. If you were a bank, you'd open more branches, or put more people in your call centre. If you were a retailer, you might seek out new, cheaper, suppliers.

Sometimes it worked and sometimes it didn't. But, in better years, there was usually enough business to go around and all but the very weak survived.

Post the global financial credit crisis, all this has now changed. Times are tougher, budgets leaner and everyone is more demanding about what they get in return for their hard-earned pound, dollar or yen.

What does that mean for business? First and foremost, it means that old adage 'if you do what you've always done, you'll get what you've always got', no longer applies. It is no longer enough to chug along making incremental improvements on what has always been done. Not even close.

Something new is required to help your team live comfortably with ambiguity. We all need to find a new way of thinking and a new way of working. Right now, not in the future, but right now.

It is not going to be easy. As I have already discussed, most companies have reacted to the fundamental shift in the global business environment by paring back staff, cutting costs and scrutinising every aspect of their business. They are apparently still resolutely following the old fall-back position of doing more things a bit better, yet now they have to do so with less people and less resources. By sticking doggedly to this old way of thinking they are actually making it harder for themselves. Worse still, they are simply buying time.

In fact, I am going to make a prediction: If companies don't change, get creative and really think on their feet, their business will die. It is simply a matter of time.

We all need to start thinking in a different, more innovative, way in order to not just survive, but grow too, in this brave new world.

There are some clues about how to do this from the past – after all if you open your eyes you can learn a lot from the successes and failures of others. Indeed, as we all know, there are some clues from the very recent past. As I write this book, I am being subjected to an almost daily diet of news about firms failing. What clues could these examples give us as to why some companies are surviving and others are falling by the wayside?

One of the companies on my radar is an old family favourite, the once trendy furnishings store Habitat. In June 2011, Habitat became just one of many retailers to collapse into administration, although three of its London stores survived.

What had this icon of Sixties style done wrong, I asked myself. After all, an item from Habitat was once a must-have fixture in every trendy urbanite's home. The answer was right there in front of me. Ironically, for an icon of creative style, Habitat did not evolve and keep up with the trends of the day. It did not innovate. It did not come up with anything new. It simply found a successful formula and went on doing more of the same, year after year. Eventually, customers got bored of it and went off to newer, more interesting pastures.

To delve further into this, I contrasted this story with a successful company. I chose Direct Line. Up until the time when Direct Line launched in 1985 with just 63 employees, consumers traditionally bought their car insurance from high street brokers. Every year, when their premium was due, people would trudge off down to their local outlet, fill in a lengthy form, wait in a queue, hand over their cash and the transaction would be complete.

Direct Line didn't want to do this. They didn't want to be like everyone else, but bigger. They decided to launch a completely new insurance model where customers bought and renewed their policies over the phone. It was a complete breath of fresh air in a business which had not changed for years. Not surprisingly, customers loved it. The company did not stop innovating either and moved on to sell online, and expanded to sell a plethora of insurance products covering everything from pets to travel to health.

First Direct mirrored Direct Line in the banking sector when they launched telephone banking in the 1980s and I, for one, have not been into a branch since. I was an early adopter and cannot speak more highly of the service and efficiency that I have enjoyed for over 20 years. These two examples were mould breaking approaches requiring creativity innovation and perseverance to make them work.

I am not suggesting that every team could come up with sector transforming ideas like these. Indeed, most won't. The point is; every organisation should be thinking in terms of how they can innovate and move forward, even if it is only via small steps. The key word here is innovation. It is not enough to just do more of the same.

Think of it another way. If someone is seriously ill in hospital, there are only so many blood transfusions and emergency operations they can have before someone eventually says; we have to switch the life support off because this is just not working.

It is the same in business; there are only so many cuts, or so much downsizing, or so many slight improvements that you can do before eventually you have to recognise this is just not working.

Creativity is not a principle that causes a team to be high performing and successful. It is, however, a key component and without it the business, as a whole, will suffer in the long term. Indeed, lack of creativity will almost certainly contribute to a long and lingering death.

This is why we need creativity in both the leadership and among all the members of our high performing teams. Creative people challenge the status quo. They constantly question the process because doing something a bit better is not good enough.

We need creativity because:

Creativity creates energy and opens doors to more enlightened futures.

When there is a diversity of creativity and a truly effective collaboration, a team will have a greater sense of energy and purpose. Get it right and the place will be buzzing!

There will be none of the usual petty point scoring common to so many teams where people guard their expertise fiercely and refuse to share the benefit of their experience. Instead, everyone will be boosted by the possibilities of what can be done when you are not just out for yourself.

Creativity allows teams to think outside the box, go beyond current boundaries and always look for better, more innovative ways to do what they are doing. A few tweaks to a process here or there is simply not good enough.

When I think about creativity I am often reminded of the well-known motivational book 'Who Moved my Cheese'[4]. For those not familiar with the thrust of the fable on which the book is based, I will try to explain. Basically, it describes four characters, two mice, Sniff and Scurry, and two little people Hem and Haw. They live in a maze where a supply of cheese is readily available and establish a routine around their daily intake of cheese. Then, one day, there is no cheese left. The two mice immediately set off to find a new supply elsewhere, but the little humans, disgusted at the lack of supply, simply starve. Eventually, realising the hopelessness of the situation, Haw starts a search for new cheese, but his friend is still dead set in his victimised mindset and does nothing.

Haw, after initially fearing the search, eventually realises that when you move beyond your own fear, it sets you

---

[4] Who Moved My Cheese? An Amazing Way to Deal with Change to Your Work and in Your Life, by Spencer Johnson. Putnam Adult 1998.

free. He becomes more and more creative in his search for the much-loved food and sure enough, eventually he is successful. After that, knowing that nothing is ever a certainty, he is constantly on the alert for new sources. He guards against getting complacent – and is duly rewarded. What is more he is energised by the whole experience.

To me there is a real moral for creativity and innovation in this story. It says; stop hanging around where you always got your cheese from because it won't always be there. Prepare yourself for this fact, accept it and go out and look!

Creativity is not….

A department!

The words 'creative' and 'creativity' in business have long been bandied about with great regularity. Over time the mere mention of the terms have obtained rather mythical, even grandiose, status. But, like most business clichés, there is usually very little understanding, or indeed will to understand, what the words actually mean.

In many cases the words are used to distance people from the job in hand. If something big needs tackling, heads of department may mutter about needing to hand it over to the 'ideas' people, as though independent thought is somehow not a discipline available to the team who carry out day-to-day tasks.

Very often, creativity is seen to be the sole domain of the marketing department. Tough tasks are kicked upstairs to these apparent ideas gurus and then effectively forgotten about because 'someone else' is taking care of the 'creativity'. Yet, no one ever seems particularly surprised when the poor souls in marketing fail to come up with a solution (notwithstanding that they are not actually in direct contact with the team that really does the job and therefore have no real understanding of the issues). It's just a 'creative problem'.

Being creative is not someone else's job. It is *our* job.

Creativity cannot be confined to one department per company, which is charged to think cleverly about anything and everything. *Everyone* should be thinking creatively. Businesses thrive on constant innovation and that needs to come from all over the company. Once you start leaving creativity up to someone else, or a different department, everyone else will be more inclined than ever to immerse themselves in their own silo and stick to the status quo. Plus, unless whatever idea is floated from afar works perfectly for each person cowering in their silo, they are more likely than ever to veto it or shout it down.

Creativity is….

Daring to think out of the box.

An acquaintance of mine is a director of a large DIY and home furnishings chain. He is a cocky little fellow, which may go some way to explaining just why he seems completely oblivious to the implications of the fundamental shifts in his sector.

Since the credit crunch, the housing market, like most others has slowed considerably. People are not buying and selling houses anymore and therefore no one is moving house. If I were this chap, I would be thinking; hang on, this looks pretty worrying. The main customers for the business are those people who have moved into their new homes and decide to completely renovate them from top to bottom. If no one is moving around, the best this home company can hope for is for customers doing little jobs in their existing homes, such as a tidy up here, or a lick of paint there. Yet, that's hardly enough to sustain a large company with many retail outlets up and down the UK.

"What are you going to do about it?" I asked him one evening over a pint.

"Well, we've been anticipating the housing slow-down for some time," he said confidently. "And, we are now going to launch a brand new range of cabinets and tools. We are also experimenting with more self assembly furniture because that seems to work quite well for IKEA."

Of course, my friend is completely missing the point. There is little point improving the cabinet range a notch. Or in bringing in other lines to ape more successful competitors. Apart from anything else, if IKEA is so good at self-assembly, just why would their customers come to this other firm?

In his haste to keep the sales figures steady for another year, my friend is focussing his energy on completely the wrong things and consoling himself that his firms figures were not as bad as his competitors! He has fallen into the trap of incremental improvements when what he should be doing is thinking creatively.

He should be asking himself and his team; what can this company do which no other home furnishings or DIY company does? How can they encourage home-owners to spend their money on houses they may have lived in for several years already?

I don't profess to have all the solutions, but with a bit of blue-sky thinking I did come up with one or two ideas. They could, for example, launch a new service where expert builders deliver and build your flat pack furniture in your home. Or, CAD technology could be deployed so customers could design their own, bespoke units and then have them professionally built for them.

These ideas may not be goers – but they are a start. This is the way that my friend, and his team should be thinking rather than looking at *small* incremental improvements to keep the firm selling its goods. They should recognise that, at present, they are on a journey which is only heading one way – and that way is down – and to him, satisfyingly not as fast as his competitors. As team leader, my friend should be leading the charge to challenge and motivate his people to think differently instead of believing only leadership has to have the answers.

There is no limit to big ideas – but you have to be prepared to think out of the box.

Finding your team's creativity

Creativity doesn't just emerge following a diktat from on high that new ideas are required this month. It is a way of life. It is the natural result of creating a workplace where people are constantly challenged and encouraged to think differently about what they are doing. As we have seen so many times in this book, high performing teams operate in an environment where people are open to any idea, no matter how mad, and are ready to try anything and everything often in the face of some quite awkward challenges.

In many ways creativity is a component that is entwined

more than any other with all the others in this book. It is impossible to create a culture that is creative unless you have:

- **Trust.** Once those on a high performing team trust their leader they will be comfortable in the knowledge that they can experiment with new ideas and concepts, however far fetched they may seem at first sight. Likewise, through a similar sense of trust in their colleagues, team members will rest assured that no one will belittle them if they drop a clanger. It is this freedom to think big that leads to innovation. Yes, there will be a few duff ideas – but without working through the bad ones, how will you ever know you have a winner? The flip-side to this is; if people are constantly looking over their shoulder in the fear that they will be punished for using their energies on anything other than the day job, progress will never be made.

- **Alignment.** A fully aligned team will quickly understand and embrace the need for creativity. This, in turn, will prompt a sense of collaboration towards the common goal so, when one member of the team is thinking their big thoughts, his or her colleagues are covering their daily tasks to ensure nothing important falls behind.

- **Attitude.** No one on a high performing team gets locked into the mindset of conformity and protecting their own silo – they all look at the bigger picture. All the time. Challenging the norms is what makes them tick – and creativity and experimentation are a big part of this.

- **Vision.** Where there is strength and a powerful purpose about what the job is and why the team is here, then there is always openness to try something new. Indeed, it not *just* an openness –

it is an eagerness to do so, if that is what is required. If a new skill is needed, or there is a need to apply a skill that has not been applied for ages, that is no problem at all. It is simply part of what needs to be done to achieve the vision. In the past, purpose has all been about self. Individual members of a team are preoccupied with how they themselves can get on. Or, how they can get a coveted pay rise or promotion. Yet, a high performing team is all about getting *everyone* to excel to get enough results to survive. Innovation is the key.

- **Rigid flexibility.** Leading edge teams are used to an environment where they can simultaneously innovate and get on with the job. In fact, they don't think there is any other way. This agility of the mind is an essential part of creativity as well as the principle of rigid flexibility

It is impossible to create a culture of innovation, purpose and creativity without addressing each one of the principles outlined here in this book. Each individual member of the team must have long-ago waved goodbye to the notion of looking after number one and have fully embraced the importance of the team. Once there is that ethic of contribution, then creativity will ensue.

The added benefit of this is; when you achieve this, creative ideas will mushroom across departments and teams. In a genuine atmosphere of collaboration one person will have no problem with passing ideas to other divisions. The concept may not have worked for them, but if there is a possibility of an effective application elsewhere, why wouldn't you pass it on?

Imagine how powerful an organisation could be if this sort of behaviour became the norm.

Imagine what could be achieved.

ABSOLUTLEY ANYTHING!

Applying creativity

In an ideal world, creativity would emanate from the whole team. In reality, even in a high performing team, creativity is always led from the top. The leader has to constantly empower the team, remind them of their sense of purpose and regularly reinforce the vision of the future. That vision will never be achieved if everyone is content to do more of the same, only better.

Good leaders will work at helping each individual member of their team recognize their own unique strengths, because each one of us is good at some things and not so strong on others. We should be able to celebrate those differences, develop those gifts and use them for the good of the company. With a bit of encouragement and positive coaching, this is not such a hard thing to do.

There needs to be an intellectual conversation as well as an emotional one with the team and that needs to be constantly reinforced. Everyone must realise that they need to be thinking innovatively and creatively about what the team is doing. Then, as each idea flows through, the team leader should remain constantly positive and encouraging. Even if at first sight something looks pretty far-fetched, the best approach is to lay off with any criticism or negative judgment. After all, if you dismiss every idea out of hand, or mock the person who came up with it, you can rest assured they'll never be back with an idea again.

Every concept should be analysed with open acceptance and appreciation.

As a leader, one area I would give particular thought to is the geographic spread of my team. Thanks to modern technology there is an increasing tendency to home working. Teams can be spread out over many miles, often only coming together once or twice a month for any face-to-face contact. This, in my mind, can really hamper creativity.

Innovation and collaboration are best fostered in an atmosphere where you can come face to face with your colleagues to kick ideas around. In the days when I used to work as a salesman, I would regularly leave my office and walk off down the corridor to find a colleague to chat with. I wasn't wasting time, or slacking. I was simply finding out what was going on around me, interacting with the people on the team and seeing what needed to be done. These conversations were very important to keep the creative juices flowing. Apart from anything else, if you don't speak to other people, how else would you ever really know what is going on, other than in your own silo?

It may not always be possible to do this today, particularly if the team is stretched across the four corners of the land. But, that doesn't mean that you shouldn't make a point of regularly talking to each other on the phone, even if there is not something vitally important and pressing to say.

If you hide behind technology such as emails, you will never get the true picture and innovative thinking will not get the free reign that it so badly needs.

One of the chief executives I coach makes a point of phoning people on his team virtually every day. He is not checking up on them, he is simply keeping an open dialogue. He asks questions such as; how was your day?, What made you laugh today? Or Spot anything interesting today? He tells me that, since he has started doing this, it is amazing what he has found out.

Creativity needs constant stimulation and to be part of the company culture in the modern era. Staff need to be motivated and to stay motivated and that is up to the team leader. That means challenging and rewarding them all in equal measure and, of course, not belittling anyone for coming up with the odd crazy idea.

At the heart of all of this is a strategy where the team leader is ever-vigilant on any area where the business is facing challenges. He or she must dedicate their energies into understanding the who, what, where and why of any given situation. They can then pass on their knowledge to those around them through regular positive communication and unleash the power of their high performing team.

Encourage everybody to keep those ideas coming – there will always be a gem in there.

Ditch the limiting mind-sets

In most instances, the key reason why teams are not creative is because, well, it is just a whole lot easier not to be so.

I once worked with a manufacturer of large-scale products for industrial use. The company was in some trouble. New product development was at a standstill, sales were dropping, quality was in free fall and morale was at rock bottom. Delving further, I discovered a raft of highly limiting mind-sets among the team. For example, the chap in charge of accessing the legal risk of the various products really couldn't care less how many they sold. In fact, if the company only sold a handful in any given month it was actually far better for him. With only a few (potentially substandard) products being installed there was less chance of him having to deal with any troublesome legal problems if anything went wrong. In fact, for him, the less products sold the better! He couldn't have cared less that the sales manager, who was charged with selling at least 50 of these products a month, was clearly way off target when only a handful were sold. He didn't see it as his problem.

My job, in coaching this dysfunctional group towards becoming a high performing team, was to create an environment where they all had a powerful sense of purpose which related to the team vision. I had to get everyone, and in particular this legal eagle, away from their silo mentality and into a collaborative culture. By them building the vision, trust, sense of purpose and acceptance of rigid flexibility, they were able to see how, by working together and improving the quality of their products, it would empower them to be more creative. Get the fundamentals right and who knows what can be achieved next?

By doing this, the legal person was able to see that the rest of the team were ensuring the products were manufactured to the highest possible specifications. He was able to relax because he was not in constant fear of legal action. Before long, he was regularly picking up the phone to the sales manager to find out how he was doing and encouraging him to keep things moving. In turn, the entire team was energised by the positive flow of energy which was now buzzing around the place, with everyone encouraging each other and pushing things forward. Ideas started flowing and the transformation in the company's fortunes was breath-taking.

Now the company was really motoring.

How creativity helps us meet our goals

One area where I have worked extensively and of which I have a great amount of personal knowledge is in financial services. My personal prediction is that this sector will see a massive shift over the next few years. However, it is the companies which are the most prepared to be creative that will be the outright winners.

Let me explain. Today, when you visit a solicitor and ask for advice, you expect to pay a fee. The same is true of an accountant. Yet, the majority of the population still do not expect to pay directly when they buy an insurance policy or a pension.

By 2013, thanks to the Financial Services Authority, we will have moved to a completely different world where once you receive your policy you will also get a bill. It is my firm belief that the Independent Financial Advisers (IFAs) that get creative, shifting the basis of their business and service most dramatically, will be the ones who will win as a result of these revolutionary changes. Yes, some top-end IFAs have been doing this for years, but for the 80 per cent that have not, this paradigm shift presents a huge opportunity. Getting it right could make all the difference between a plunge in their new business turnover and soaring profits. Creativity of thought is the key.

The key points to recall from creativity are:

- To handle ambiguity with ease then we have to deploy creativity in order to find fresh and workable ways
- Creativity is not the responsibility of leadership alone, some of the best ideas come from the periphery where real people are executing the job
- For Teams to move towards high performing then 'things need to change' and that is where creativity will help
- Leader, take responsibility for asking questions of your Team Members daily that might lead to learning of different ways of doing things.

Chapter eleven - Credibility

While I was in the senior team at Abbey Life, the then Team Leader decided that we needed to give the sales division a bit of a boost. The year was 1980 and the 2000 strong salesforce was doing OK, but were not achieving anything particularly spectacular. The salesforce consisted of the usual mix of salespeople, a combination of total stars who would do well whatever the economic climate and those who were content to just plod along, but always brought in adequate results. In fact, they were pretty much like any sales team, in any firm, anywhere. And that was the problem. We wanted something much better.

After much discussion, it was decided to run an internal competition to give a better ending to the final four months of the year. To make it fair, there would have to be something in it for everyone so the stars did not run away with all the prizes. We wanted some sort of mechanic built into the system so even the lowest producer would win points and end up with an incentive.

Half a million pounds was allocated to this promotion, which, as you can see, was no small sum, particularly considering it was more than thirty years ago. It is easy to understand that with something this significant we needed professional help and we called in a number of promotions companies to pitch for the business.

On the day of the pitch we heard one presentation after another. The companies we had invited in had pulled out all the stops because clearly, as I have already said, this was a substantial piece of business. However, one pitch stood out head and shoulders above the rest. The presentation was flawless, the ideas for the competition were breathtakingly original and they had also added in all sorts of other fancy ideas for stuff they could do on top of the main competition for no extra cost. Every single senior person from this big name promotions company was on hand to make the presentation and drive home their superior credentials. They even brought along a very glamorous tall blond model to hold up the presentation boards. Well, it was the 1980s!

The final bone this promotions agency threw in our direction was an invitation for the senior Abbey Life team to take advantage of their corporate hospitality at a very exclusive forthcoming social event. Now you know where the politicians got their ideas from!

Everyone at Abbey Life who was there that day was impressed.

How could we all fail to be anything but bowled over by this display? The promotions giant was duly appointed and we sat back in eager anticipation to watch the magic unfold.

What happened next, or rather didn't happen at all, turned out to be one of the biggest disappointments of my corporate life. Yes, the competition was run, it produced the desired results, the team was duly motivated and our sales showed a marginal rise for the end of the financial year. But, that was it.

We never saw those senior people from the promotions company again. They never even picked up the phone to see how things were going. Instead we were left with a handful of junior staff to manage the finer points of the competition.

What was even more galling though was that none of the bells and whistles that we were promised – those extra ideas of what they could do on top of the main competition at no cost – ever saw the light of day. Perhaps this was a consequence of the lack of experience of these young promotions executives, who were handling the account, or maybe they were not even told about the ideas, or perhaps it was our naivety. Either way, they were never mentioned again. The corporate hospitality did not materialise either, but that was by the by.

At the end of the competition, there was a palpable sense of disappointment among the senior team. We had been given a Saatchi & Saatchi-style pitch, but a Bloggs & Co delivery. It was, as we could clearly see, all flannel.

I am not relating this simply to get it off my chest. It is to me the perfect example of the importance of credibility in a high performing team. Credibility is a rich combination of intent, integrity, competence and results. While the sales promotion team adequately (though not spectacularly) fulfilled the latter two elements of this list, they were way off the first two. We did not get anything close to what we were promised which clearly calls their intent and integrity into question.

The sales promotion giant did not therefore have any credibility.

Is this important? You bet it is.

If you asked me then if I would ever use this promotions company again, my immediate answer would be; no, never. In fact, I still wouldn't use them today – and I am sure none of my colleagues from back then would either.

Credibility is important. People often mistake credibility for simply getting good results. It isn't. It is, as we can see here, very much about intent, integrity and competence too. If teams do not get all these elements right, those on the receiving end of their service will feel disgruntled, fed-up and generally inclined to go elsewhere in the future. They may not even be able to put their finger on what it is that is upsetting them. They'll just know that the gulf between their expectation and what they got is unacceptably wide.

Do you want people to be thinking that about your team? Of course not. Now is the time to think about the credibility of your high performing team.

We need credibility because:

A team that has credibility is, quite simply, easier to follow and easier to support. If your team exudes credibility – people *want* to decide in your favour. Those outside the firm will trust that what you say is not simply 'noise' about impending results; it is a real-time update. They'll know this because of your unblemished record of high integrity, skills and competencies which are entirely relevant to your team's purpose. Therefore they will be quick to support you and open to hearing your ideas.

Think about it. Let's say you are a supplier to a large multinational catalogue company. You've not had the business long and your people and their people are just starting to feel their way and begin forming relationships. There will inevitably be all the usual 'them and us' frictions; the supplier being eager to please, the larger company expecting excellent service. How would you cement that relationship?

The answer is, of course, by doing the job properly (getting results), but also by going the extra mile and proving that you are the firm to get things done honestly, efficiently and on time (showing your intent, integrity and competence). Whatever the challenge, brutal honesty must pertain no matter what might be testing it.

Once you have established this relationship and proved your credibility, what would happen if you the supplier thought of a new, potentially lucrative, target market for the mailing house? It is an idea which could prove lucrative for you both. Do you think that the larger company would be more receptive, or less receptive to hearing your ideas now you have proved your credibility? Clearly they'd be more receptive.

That is the value of credibility. Trust me, it will open doors that were not open to you before. Plus, if the ground work has been laid, our fictitious supplier will not have to spend hours and hours preparing an in depth presentation to its client (a presentation where half the pages won't ever be read too). They'll simply be able to open and honest conversation with the catalogue giant. If you've already proved your worth, you won't have to keep reinventing the wheel.

This, of course, works both ways.

Whilst writing this book there is one particular team that I am working with who are very frustrated over their credibility. Or perceived *lack* of credibility by its shareholders who are constantly challenging what they say.

The fact is, when I first met this team six months earlier, they were not doing very well and had not been for some time. When I first went to see them they were forecasting a loss in the low seven figures.

Since then though, a lot has changed. The team has made significant cuts in personnel and systems to address their losses. They have aligned behind a simple plan and begun to address some limiting mindsets. In fact, their activity and positive interdependent working has blossomed wildly in a remarkably short space of time. Everyone on the team agrees that they are enjoying work much more, a fact backed up by a monthly survey which demonstrates big improvements in morale, and the icing on the cake is the firm is on the verge of some very big breakthroughs in results which will have a substantial impact on the bottom line.

Fantastic, you might say. What's the problem?

Well, the problem is, those at Group HQ of the firm are profoundly cynical about these leaps forward. Shareholders have heard it all before. After all, what company when it is in trouble, would not promise 'jam tomorrow'? Most firms sail along in splendour, promising all and sundry that things are going brilliantly, right up until the moment that it is abundantly clear that this is not the case. This firm was no different. Now, when they declare that everything is going pretty well actually, it is hardly surprising that no one is exactly jumping off their chair to congratulate them. The shareholders are judging the team on the basis of poor past results together with a clear lack of integrity because they never faced up to their problems. Right now, there is no visible proof of the improvements in results and therefore nothing to convince any stakeholders.

It is not enough for this team to sort out their internal problems and get their figures back on track. If they want to quiet the naysayers and get the external support they need to get fully back on track, this team has to work on their credibility. In effect, they have to start again to convince outsiders of their intent and integrity. What they must do more of at this stage is to improve the communication regarding their currently changed approach – their intent and integrity.

Someone once said that the road to heaven is paved with good intentions. I'd say that the road to credibility is paved with competence, healthy intentions and proof in the pudding.

Credibility is not about….

Results!

Picture the scenario. Team A is getting a new senior widget analyst. The chap is due to start in two weeks. His colleagues, curious about their soon-to-be team mate, ask the team leader what this fellow is like.

"Oh, he is perfect," the team leader will reply with enthusiasm.

"He used to be the senior widget analyst at Blue Chip Company PLC."

This sort of answer will satisfy most people. Indeed, it will most likely impress them too. But, look beyond the superficial fact that he used to work at the biggest company in your field, and what have you got? After all, he may only have been a senior widget analyst at Blue Chip for a matter of months. He may have 'left suddenly' under a cloud. The bulk of this new recruit's career (and the bit of which he believes he achieved the most and of which he is the most proud) may have even been at Small Insignificant Company Ltd.

The point is – you can never truly judge a person's credibility by results. At best, the headline figures tell you very little at all. At worst, they are downright misleading.

Unfortunately, most people equate credibility with one single indicator – results. It happens in all walks of life, all the time, but judging someone by their results is very poor indicator indeed.

If your credibility is solely based on results, what happens when you have a bad month? Or a bad couple of months? Or when you don't quite pull off a massive new business pitch? Your credibility will come into question. Others will start to wonder whether you are really up to the job, or if they should be working with you, or your team. You and your team will only ever be as good as your last sales figures, or account win, or year-end results.

In fact, you will end up in just the same scenario as the team I mentioned above. You might lose the confidence of your stakeholders because you are not achieving the results.

This team's experience is not a rare one either. It happens everywhere. Most of the organisations where I have ever worked unconsciously measure credibility on the results that the team produces. Indeed, when I held a sales directors role many years ago, the only time my credibility was called into question by my peers was the one year in seven when we did not exceed the previous year's figures by over 25 per cent.

It is a pattern I see repeated time again since I have been coaching teams too. I am, for example, currently working with another company with very similar issues. This firm, a large international, business-to-business, company with offices just outside London, has a global chief executive who is only interested in the bottom line. It is the only aspect of the business that ever worries him. He is of the mindset that if the company has a bad week he is literally looking around the room to see how many staff he can shed on the Friday.

In the case of this business-to-business company, I am working with the UK general manager. Can you imagine how frustrating it is for him to be constantly under threat of losing a swathe of his best people, because the figures are not quite up-to-scratch for that period? I know, from my work with him and the UK team, that the UK side of this business is now pretty darn close to becoming a high performing team. As a result of their sterling efforts over the past few months, they are in-line to win some substantial new business contracts too. Yet, on an almost daily basis, this general manager is being forced to explain himself to ward off any cut-backs from his impatient international pay masters. The global chief executive is completely ignoring the intent and integrity of this smart hard-working team.

Clearly at some stage this team, like any other, does have to deliver the results. Once concrete examples of the firm's undoubted improvement are in, the general manager can rest assured that his boss will be off his back. Sadly, I don't think there is much they can do to change the situation until then.

My advice to the general manager would be that, once the results are in, he should use the opportunity to convey the importance of other aspects of credibility such as intent and integrity. That is that; the checks and balances are in place to ensure future success.

His blandishments will no longer fall on deaf ears and this is the opportunity to 'retrain' his boss that results are not the be all and end all.

He could say something like: "Do you remember when I made that presentation last year? I said I had doubled the amount of meetings we were having with new prospects from eight to 16, per month? Well, as we said at the time, our intention was always to see more people and spread our brand wider than ever before. This is the fruit of that intent."

The subtext is, of course: "Next time we tell you something like this – trust us as a credible team!"

We all have a duty to educate all those around us that there is more to credibility than just the bottom line. Once there is trust and understanding that you will do what you said you will do, it is to everyone's advantage.

An important part of my work with the business-to-business team, and indeed any of the teams I work with, is to instil a greater understanding throughout the organization of the breadth of credibility. There is, after all, no way that teams can sustain high performance indefinitely without comprehending the values, intent and behaviours that create sustainable credibility.

Credibility is….

A balanced combination of:

- Intent
- Integrity
- Competence

Results

- **Intent**
  Based on the team's motives, agenda and resulting behaviour. When all three are based on honesty and mutual interest, trust in the team's performance will ensue.
- **Integrity**
  Sticking to moral and ethical principles, alongside soundness of character and honesty. Team members with integrity will stand for something, make and keep commitments to themselves and will stick to their guns in the face of even the most challenging circumstances. *
- **Competence**
  The talent, attitude, skills and knowledge that are required to deliver results. Good capable teams know everyone's strengths *and* their weaknesses and work together to compensate for them and keep themselves relevant. *
- **Results**
  Getting the job done, or exceeding expectations, offers a visible, tangible and measurable proof of credibility that can be evaluated by others. [5]

Results are, as you can see, a key component of credibility. However, they are not the be all and end all. It is just as important that a team is honest in the way it sets and accomplishes objectives, keeps commitments and 'walks the talk'.

The supporting values of intent, integrity and competence

---

[5] The Great Workplace. Michael Burchell and Jennifer Robin. Jossey Bass

are what show that a team is reliable and credible. These values frame the strategy as well as the creativity and innovation of the team. They are just as important as results when it comes to assessing how effective and impactful a team might be.

Each component is as important as the other. If, for example, there is a gap between intent and integrity, it upsets those on the receiving end. It often upsets them in a way they don't actually declare, perhaps because they can't totally put their finger on what it is that is disturbing them. It may be simply a feeling, but that unsettled feeling is usually a good sign that credibility is being questioned. The worst part about this is; if people don't complain when they feel like this, you won't be able to do anything about it. The first you will know about it is when a customer doesn't return.

It is therefore vital to have a clear understanding and appreciation of all four components.

Don't forget too, if you manage to give your team credibility through the combination of these elements, it will give you some breathing room when things don't immediately go to plan. Others will recognize that the team has always been true to its word and won't be so quick to judge simply on the basis of results.

Finding your team's credibility

Quite often, when I discuss the deep importance of credibility with the teams I work with, they become so keen to do something about it that they include it in their team values. This is great and I would not discourage it. It certainly highlights the importance of credibility in the overall scheme of things and will encourage the team to strive towards their vision while carefully complying with the demands of integrity, intent and competence.

It might help, however, if we take one step backwards to break down what credibility means in action. To begin the journey towards credibility in your high performing team, start by identifying the factors that help or hinder this vital component.

Which tendencies do your team, both individually and collectively, mostly display? Answer honestly.

Increase Credibility	Reduces Credibility
Confident demeanour	Hesitant manner
Clear intentions constantly displayed	Apparent hidden agenda
Readiness to be personally responsible and accountable	Quick to shift blame to others or cite troublesome 'outside' factors
Calm, straight talking	Beating around the bush and spin
Expectations discussed with clarity	Willingness to create or accept false assumptions
Eagerness to address the important issues first	Tendency to sidestep principle problems
Care for the position of others and understanding of their viewpoint	Disregard for alternative views, with clearly only thought for themselves.

Once there is an understanding of where your team sits on the 'credibility scale', understanding the adjustments that are required and then making them becomes more straight forward.

Getting ready to apply that credibility

It will probably come as no surprise to you to read that credibility, like so many of the traits which lead to a high performing team, emanates straight from the top. If a leader is strong in terms of intent, integrity and competence and the team is consistently getting results, this will automatically lift the level of credibility within the team. Therefore, according to the list above, what we are looking for is a straight-talking, decisive and accountable leader, who is sensitive to the viewpoint of others.

It is incumbent on the person at the top to adjust their behaviour to meet these targets, if he or she feels they are falling short in any way.

If they are successful in doing so, this will bear fruit because a leader that is confident and is delivering on his or her promises (and doing so with aplomb), will inspire supportive feedback from the team. This feedback will, in turn, oil the wheels of progress and influence the behaviour of those in the ranks below. Pretty soon everyone will be addressing issues head on, airing their intentions clearly and working together confidently, as it is human nature to emulate behaviour at the top.

Credibility is not a one shot deal either. The leader doesn't just put on a bold face, invite the troops to follow him over the top and then that is the job done. Like all the components of a high performing team, it has to be part of the day-to-day way of life in the company.

High performing teams need credibility from the top to the bottom, but the impetus needs to come from above. The leader needs to demonstrate the four characteristics of credibility constantly and visibly. All the time be encouraging it from each of the individuals on the Team.

If this does not happen and a leader is wavering or unsure, or promises the earth, but delivers little, it will lead to a downward spiral of events. The team may receive an increase in their workload so they can achieve the results that the dithering leader is unable to achieve (yet mistakenly believes is the *only* route to credibility). Then, in the long, or even medium term, this will sap the energy of the team and erode any credibility it already had.

One of the most obvious examples of credibility gone wrong, and good intentions not being sustained – and one of my personal pet hates – is when you hear a senior member of staff bad mouthing a colleague behind their backs. We've all seen it and heard it done. I bet we are all thinking the same thing when we hear it too:

If you are saying this about Jim/Sarah when they are not around, I bet you say the same thing about the rest of the team and probably even me when our backs are turned.

Clearly this gossipy leader, in a bid to be one of the lads, is not taking into account the values of the team, the ramifications of what they are saying and the knock on effects of the way they are demonstrating their intention. That leader has no credibility.

As I said – we all know teams like this and they are not high performing. Not even close.

Ditch the limiting mind-sets

The traditional leadership style in most (non high performing) teams is to resort to the carrot and stick approach to achieve their goals. If a colleague does well – and gets results – they will be praised and if they fall short, they'll be in the dog house. They may even be in a position of losing their job.

Clearly the limiting mind-set here is the widely held belief that if you get results you automatically win credibility. However, as we have seen, there is more to credibility than pushing and bullying to get results. Besides which, if a firm resolutely continues down this path they eventually won't have any staff left because it is virtually impossible to get top results time after time. Colleagues will either be pushed out, or will more likely leave in droves of their own volition because of the pressure of unrealistic and unsupported expectations.

Imagine how different things would be if, instead of constantly focussing on results, the person on top was also keen to hear about their colleagues' intent. How are they going to go about getting those results? What is it that they need to do their job? Are there any problems that others can help that person overcome?

In an atmosphere like this, it may be that the leader can see a better, more satisfactory, or more efficient way to get to the end result. Then, because there is an environment of honest, open discussion, with none of the inappropriate pressure that surrounds a results-orientated mentality, both parties can decide the best way to go forward. At a stroke the credibility of the team will reach a new level.

Ditching the limiting mind-set of a focus on pure results will help in a range of other situations too. Picture, for example, an interview scenario. As I pointed out earlier, most people have a tendency to highlight their spell with Blue Chip Company PLC, as a shorthand to prove their great value. If the interviewer is inclined to link credibility with pure results, it is likely that they will be swayed by this even if they have a niggling feeling at the back of their mind that this person does not seem right. This is, of course, the way that terrible recruitment mistakes occur.

If, on the other hand, the interviewer understands that credibility is a broader subject, combining qualities such as integrity and intent, as well as results, they are far more likely to probe more deeply. They are more likely to push the fellow from Blue Chip with some smart behavioural questioning to find out what work he is proud of, or where he felt he fell short. Now they'd be getting somewhere.

Understanding the importance of credibility, and accepting its wider meaning instead of focussing on the limiting mind-set of pure results, will benefit a high performing team hugely. It says so much about your business and the way you do business. It is what makes people believe in you and what makes a high performing team believe in each other.

How credibility helps us to reach our goals

Applied carefully, credibility can even save your business. A few years back, I worked with a financial services team which dealt with contracts worth billions of pounds. Two years before the global financial crisis hit, this team underwent a process where they streamlined their previously complex processes with the intent of making the decision making and authority from the main board easier and faster. Although they had no way of knowing what was coming with the credit crisis – or the extent of it – their previous work on their processes ensured that their credibility was already high when the crisis unfolded. As a result, they were able to respond magnificently. In my mind there is not a shadow of doubt that their positioning protected that team from potentially awful circumstances that brought down many other previously magnificent firms. The credibility of the team at this financial services company is what saved the day and perhaps even saved the entire organisation, not to put too fine a point on it.

The key points to take from credibility are:

- Credibility allows us space and time to get on with the job without interference
- Sharing and communicating intention, diligent process and integrity are all keys to establishing individual and team credibility
- Credibility in the eyes of all your stakeholders is energising. It creates a positive place to work and is imperative when it comes to 4+4= more than 8
- Holding people accountable for their work output strengthens everyone's credibility – especially yours and that of your team.

Team Leaders Responsibility

While I was writing this book, I gave a few chapters to some trusted friends and clients to see what they thought. I invited them to be totally honest and not hold back in voicing their true opinions.

One of my 'reviewers', a managing director of a medium-sized firm who I had not worked with for long, gave me an interesting and unexpected reaction.

"Yes, this is great, but it is missing an important point," he mused. "I can see the value in all of this and would love to have such a high performing team but the problem is, I am too soft.

"I know that I should be a lot firmer with my team. There is at least one person who really shouldn't be with us at all. I'm finding it difficult to do anything about it though."

My client has made a very important point and it is one that troubles many people who lead teams. Fundamentally, it is human nature to want to be liked and to exist in a harmonious environment. Yet, the corollary to this is the fact that, to achieve a high performing team, a leader will constantly need to stick his or her neck out and really lead. They will have to ask their subordinates to do things that may not immediately appear easy or straightforward. They will have to change the company culture, even though initially most people will be highly resistant.

In short, they will have to put the needs for the greater good of the team above their own popularity.

My client is not alone in his hesitancy to do the right thing. I come across many people who are quite au fait with the theory, but apparently fail at the last (arguably most important) hurdle, which is putting it into practice.

What makes it worse, is they are usually only too aware that they are doing it thanks to that helpful quality that we all possess – intuition. Intuition, or 'gut feeling' is the product of our education, our previous experiences and a little dash of something from our deeper consciousness.

Business leaders often swear by it in the decision-making process for negotiating deals.

So, why is it that so many ignore it when it comes to their dealings with their teams? After going through the theory here, many people may have easily been able to spot the internal terrorists I have talked about so much. In fact, it is more than likely that they had niggling doubts about this character long before. The problem is, just like my client, they hesitate.

None of this is to say that creating a high preforming team is all about firing a couple of trouble-makers and banging some heads together. It is merely to point out that to create a high performing team, you have to get started and do something. Then, once you have started, you have to keep going. Don't ignore the 'harder bits' because you don't want to upset your colleagues. Similarly, don't ignore your intuition when something is nagging away at the base of your skull telling you something is not working.

It is very easy to get into the habit of letting things ride. If everything else seems to be going along OK, why rock the boat if just a few elements don't seem to be falling into place? However, if you have set out on the journey, this is exactly what you should be doing. All the time. Challenge everything, but challenge it constructively.

Once you start working this way, things will start to fall into place. I guarantee it.

Take, for example, the lessons learned about vision in chapter one. All being well, having read this, you will focus on your vision and communicate it to your eager team.

What happens though, if you go out into the workforce, ask them what they think of it and they say; they didn't really get it? Do you ignore it because it seems like hard work to keep going though it? Tell them to work a bit harder to understand it? Or, do you find a different way of communicating it to them?

You should, of course, find another way of expressing it to help them see the vision as you do. It may take a bit of hard work and dedication, but it's vital to never lose sight of why you are doing it in the first place.

The best thing is, if the team is telling you they don't get it, it is actually a sign of great progress. They haven't merely paid lip service to the 'latest initiative' and nodded to say; 'yes boss, great idea'. They can see that it is important and that their full understanding is required. And, they have had the guts to say they don't quite get it. That is progress indeed.

As a team leader you have to learn to be a bit of a juggler too. Although this book is broken down into chapters addressing each of the principles and characteristics, it is not something to be followed sequentially. There is no use in 'doing' vision, ticking that off and moving on to plan and purpose. Each element is important and must be pursued at the same time. It is quite likely that one principle will be more important than another at any given time and that balance will change in an instant. What is important is that you always keep this in your mind and are alert and ready to tackle the critically important elements as and when they are needed.

Creating a high performing team is an endeavour that requires constant attention. If you will allow me one final sporting analogy, I would say that it is vital to remember that just because a team played brilliantly this weekend, does not mean they will do the same thing again next weekend. Different circumstances will arise and the players will react in different ways to them. Indeed, they may well react in a different way to entirely the same set of circumstances.

There is little point in setting out on this journey to create a high performing team unless you constantly follow it through and are prepared to react to new challenges. Plus, even if something seems to be working just fine, you must endeavour to keep going back to it and making sure it is still OK. Things can and do change all the time.

If you are serious about creating a high performing team, you will be embarking on a process and this process will demand your constant attention at all times to help it to succeed. It requires that you listen to your intuition and use your core abilities to their fullest. It will not be a smooth, linear journey and may take some time. The important thing is to never give up. If you do this, you will succeed in creating the high performing team you truly deserve. What a great feeling would that be?

Good luck!

Appendix

Further reading

For further reading on teams, I recommend some key authors on team building. The first is Reilly and Jones[6] list of four essential elements of teams which they list as: goals, interdependence, commitment and accountability.

- The members must have *mutual goals or a reason* to work together.
- There must be an *interdependent working relationship*
- Individuals must be *committed* to the group effort.
- The group must be *accountable* to a higher level within the organisation.

The overall objective of a work team is to exercise control over organisational change. Functionally, this involves *increased* decision-making and problem-solving efforts, although a side effect may be to increase the productivity of individual members. A primary objective of team building is to increase awareness of group process. In essence, the group members must learn how to control change *externally* by experimenting *internally*. The team-building effort will concentrate on barriers to effective functioning and the selection of strategies to overcome these barriers.

The individual is, therefore, the vital component of a high performing team.

---

[6] 1974

Organisational failures often are not a result of poor leadership but of poor followership from the ranks below. Few training programmes teach people how to be an effective member of a democratic group.

To be an effective team member a person needs to:

- Understand and be committed to group goals
- Be friendly, concerned and interested in others
- Acknowledge and confront conflict openly
- Listen to others with understanding
- Include others in the decision making process
- Recognise and respect individual differences
- Contribute and respect individual differences
- Value the ideas and contributions of others
- Recognise and reward team efforts
- Encourage and appreciate comments about team performance

These characteristics are in a sequential pattern, alternating task and relationship behaviours. This pattern of behaviour is the starting point for the development of a model of team building. It is helpful to explore this model here, because it forms the backbone to the six principles in the first part of this book.

A model of team building

The model of team building presented by Chuck Kormanski and Andrew Mozenter (1987), is in accord with Tuckman's (1977) five stages of group development: forming, storming, norming, performing and adjourning. The model is sequential, developmental and thematic as are most theories of group development. The model is sequential in that there are five stages that occur in order;

each stage has a general theme that describes group activity. The developmental nature of the model requires that the theme activities be accomplished and problems resolved at each stage before movement to the next stage. The model includes behaviours that are task oriented and relationship oriented and it reflects the elements and characteristics of team presented earlier. Therefore, if you would like to consider it in the context of your own team, you may want to take into account activities over the last three years, as well as where you are now.

A model of team building

Stage	Theme	Task Outcome	Relationship Outcome
One – Forming	Awareness	Commitment	Acceptance
Two – Storming	Conflict	Clarification	Belonging
Three – Norming	Cooperation	Involvement	Support
Four – Performing	Productivity	Achievement	Pride
Five - Adjourning	Separation	Recognition	Satisfaction

The five themes and their respective task and relationship outcomes are as follows:

- **Awareness** (commitment and acceptance)
- **Conflict** (clarification and belonging)
- **Cooperation** (involvement and support)
- **Productivity** (recognition and satisfaction)
- **Separation** (recognition and satisfaction)

Stage One: Awareness

The forming stage of group development involves the task objective of becoming oriented and the relationship objective of resolving dependencies. Awareness is an overall theme. Team members need to understand and become committed to group goals and to be friendly, concerned and interested in others. Individuals must begin by getting acquainted with one another. The unique identities and personal skills of individuals are important resources to be shared in order to create feelings of acceptance.

However, getting acquainted is not enough; there are many groups in which the members feel comfortable with one another and know one another's strengths and weaknesses yet accomplish nothing. Therefore, the initial task activity is setting goals. This gives meaning to the team's existence. Not only do individuals need to understand how the team fits within the organisation, they also need to understand how they are related to the team's goals.

The desired outcomes for the first stage are commitment and acceptance. These outcomes are critical to team development and are prerequisites to movement to the next stage.

Stage Two: Conflict

The storming stage of group development involves the task objective of resistance and the relationship objective of resolving feelings of hostility. Conflict emerges naturally. Team-building behaviours at this stage include acknowledging and confronting conflict openly at the task level and listening with understanding to others at the relationship level. Desired outcomes in this stage are clarification and belonging.

It is important that individuals listen attentively and actively to all viewpoints at this stage. The diversity of opinions shared provides the team with a vital source of group energy. Team members become responsible for developing an atmosphere that encourages and supports the expression of opinions and fosters a sense of belonging. By encouraging expression of all disagreement and dealing with it, a team further clarifies its purpose begins to define its most effective means for working together.

Stage Three: Cooperation

The norming stage of group development involves the task objective of promoting open communication and the relationship objective of increasing cohesion. The overall theme is one of cooperation. Appropriate behaviours for team members are including others in the decision-making process (task) and recognising and respecting individual differences (relationship). The desired outcomes for teams in the third stage are involvement and support.

As collaboration becomes a team norm, a feeling of genuine support develops. Members are more able to give and receive feedback. As the giving and receiving of feedback increases within the team, members have a better understanding of where they stand and become more involved in decision making.

Stage Four: Productivity

The performing stage of group development involves the task objective of solving problems and the relationship objective of promoting interdependence. The general theme is productivity.

Team members are encouraged to contribute ideas and solutions and to value the contributions and ideas of others. Desired outcomes for this stage are achievement and pride.

In team building, members work collaboratively to achieve desired goals and objectives. In successful teams, members are challenged to work to their greatest potential in order to do this. A major concern at this stage is sustaining momentum and enthusiasm. Complex goals and objectives require the creation of incremental steps and sub-goals. The establishment of milestones or benchmarks for success at such points and the celebration when these points are reached contribute both to motivation and team revitalisation.

Stage Five: Separation

The adjourning stage of group development may occur for groups that have a specified lifetime. It also may occur when a major task is completed or when new team members are added. Some on-going teams do not conclude at the fifth stage but recycle from stage five to stage one without adjourning.

During stage five, the task objective is recognising and rewarding team efforts and the relationship objective stresses encouraging and appreciating team performance.

The desired outcomes of the final stage of team building are recognition and satisfaction.

For those groups that are adjourning, an evaluation of team accomplishments provides important feedback regarding job performance and working relationships. This documentation of team history can be used to plan future ventures involving other teams. This also provides a sense of closure for the group and allows individuals to either say goodbye or commit to a future of further collaboration. This stage is, in essence, a final celebration that includes both recognition and satisfaction. So where are we now?

The figure that follows presents an integration of group-development theory and the team-building model described here. For each of the five stages of Tuckman's model, task and relationship behaviour is noted, a general theme is identified and both task and relationship team-building outcomes are listed.

Why we need transformational skills

Selznick (1957) first suggests the importance of transformational skills as critical components of dynamic leadership, but it is Burns (1978) who provides a thorough introduction to them.

In the awareness stage of the team-development model, the transformational skills needed to encourage commitment and acceptance are value clarification, visioning (identifying mission and purpose) and communicating through myth and metaphor (using stories and anecdotes to describe philosophy and define culture). During the conflict stage, the skills of flexibility (developing openness and versatility), creativity and kaleidoscopic thinking (discovering new ways of viewing old problems) will assist with the development, clarification and belonging. The cooperation stage requires the skills of playfulness and humour, entrepreneurship and networking (building coalitions of support). At the productivity stage, the skills of multicultural awareness, mentoring and futuring (forecasting outcomes through trend analysis) help to create achievement and pride. The last stage, separation requires the skills of celebrating (using ceremony to acknowledge accomplishment) and closure to promote recognition and satisfaction.

The skills essential for successful team development are both simple and complex. They are used by both team leaders and team members. One set (transaction) aids in efficient management and the other (transformational) promotes effective leadership. The following figure depicts the skills that are used predominantly in each stage of team development.

Team Building Skills

Stage of Team Development	Task and Relationship Outcome	Transactional Skills (Management)	Transformational Skills (Leadership)
1 Awareness Forming	Commitment and acceptance	Getting acquainted, goal setting, organising	Value clarification, visioning, communication through myth and metaphor
2 Conflict Storming	Clarification and belonging	Active listening, assertiveness, conflict management	Flexibility, creativity, kaleidoscopic thinking
3 Cooperation Norming	Involvement and support	Communicating, feedback, affirmation	Playfulness and humour, entrepreneuring, networking
4 Productivity Performing	Achievement and pride	Decision making, problem solving, rewarding	Multicultural awareness, mentoring, futuring
5 Separation Adjoining	Recognition and satisfaction	Evaluation, reviewing	Celebrating, bringing closure

Lightning Source UK Ltd.
Milton Keynes UK
UKHW010836181120
373613UK00001B/55